WELCOME TO UEFA EURO 2024

ALEKSANDER ČEFERIN
UEFA PRESIDENT

Since its kick-off in 1960, the European Football Championship has become one of the planet's most thrilling sports events. This summer's edition has more than lived up to that billing, with 24 teams contributing to a wonderful festival of football as they aimed to make history and lift the much-desired Henri Delaunay trophy.

Famous for its rich footballing heritage, Germany has provided the perfect stage to host UEFA EURO 2024, a joyous occasion for players, officials and fans alike.

This summer's tournament has celebrated not just the skill and virtue of the protagonists on the field but also life, inclusion, and diversity.

UEFA, the German Football Association (DFB), and federal and local government structures have united to deliver an event honouring democracy, respect, tolerance, and human rights. We have taken significant steps to minimise the tournament's environmental impact and established a climate fund for grassroots football, which promises a lasting legacy.

I want to thank everyone involved, from our sponsors and partners to suppliers, for your incredible support and unwavering dedication to our mission.

Now, let's enjoy the final acts of this magical summer of football in a spirit of fair play and respect, creating yet more unforgettable memories together.

Let's be united by football!

Seit ihrer ersten Ausgabe im Jahr 1960 hat sich die Fußball-Europameisterschaft zu einem der weltweit bekanntesten und spannendsten Sportereignisse hervorgetan. Das war diesen Sommer nicht anders – 24 Mannschaften sind angetreten, um den begehrten Henri-Delaunay-Pokal zu gewinnen, und haben uns ein denkwürdiges Fußballfest bereitet.

Gastgeber Deutschland, eine Fußballnation sondergleichen, bot die perfekte Bühne für die UEFA EURO 2024 und ihre Hauptakteure – die Spieler, Offiziellen und Fans. Das Turnier hat nicht nur das Können der Akteure, sondern auch die verschiedensten Aktivitäten abseits des Spielfelds rund um Inklusion und Vielfalt in den Fokus gerückt.

Die UEFA, der Deutsche Fußball-Bund (DFB) sowie die Bundesregierung, die Landesregierungen und die Städte haben gemeinsam eine Veranstaltung auf die Beine gestellt, die als Vorbild für Demokratie, Respekt, Toleranz und Menschenrechte gilt. Wir haben weitreichende Maßnahmen ergriffen, um die die Auswirkungen des Turniers auf die Umwelt zu minimieren, und einen Klimafonds für den Breitenfußball aufgelegt, der über den Sommer hinaus ein nachhaltiges Vermächtnis hinterlässt.

Ich möchte allen Beteiligten, von unseren Sponsoren und Partnern bis hin zu unseren Zulieferern, für ihr herausragendes Engagement und die tatkräftige Unterstützung unserer Arbeit danken.

Lassen Sie uns nun die letzten Akte dieses magischen Fußballsommers im Sinne von Fairplay und Respekt genießen und gemeinsam noch mehr unvergessliche Erinnerungen schaffen.

United by Football. Vereint im Herzen Europas.

WELCOME *ALL*

Everyone has a place in football

#FOOT*BALL*

UEFA

WILLKOMMEN IN DEUTSCHLAND

BERND NEUENDORF
DFB PRESIDENT

This summer, after a 36-year hiatus, Germany and the German Football Association have once again hosted a European Championship – all over Germany this time. Back in 1988, the only other time the European Championship was held here, our country was still divided. This year, alongside newcomers Dortmund in the west, and Leipzig and Berlin in the east, a total of ten cities have hosted the event. After weeks of incredible matches, our united Germany is now looking forward to the all-important semi-finals and, of course, the final.

UEFA EURO 2024 has once again proved that Germany is a football-loving nation. The unifying power of our sport has been felt everywhere this summer, since the very first day of the tournament. In the stadiums and on the fan miles, supporters from all over the world have met and celebrated football peacefully together. We have witnessed some impressive fan marches and a cheerful and exuberant atmosphere in the host cities. Millions of people have also followed their teams on TV – cheering, celebrating and crying. That's the beauty of football.

UEFA EURO 2024 will have an impact long after the final, not only because of the lasting memories created by the outstanding teams and unique atmosphere, but because the tournament has also brought sustainability to the fore and given amateur football a real boost in a variety of ways.

All that remains if for me to wish you, and indeed all of us, some fantastic semi-finals and an unforgettable final, replete with exciting football and inspiring encounters both inside and outside the stadiums.

Nach 36 Jahren durften Deutschland und der Deutsche Fußball-Bund in diesem Sommer wieder eine Europameisterschaft ausrichten – und zwar in ganz Deutschland. 1988, als die Europameisterschaft zum bisher einzigen Mal in Deutschland stattfand, war unser Land noch geteilt. In diesem Jahr zählten – neben dem Neuling Dortmund im Westen – Leipzig und Berlin im Osten erstmals zu unseren insgesamt zehn EM-Spielorten. Das wiedervereinte Deutschland freut sich nach großartigen Turnierwochen nun auf die finalen großen Highlights.

Die UEFA EURO 2024 hat einmal mehr unter Beweis gestellt, dass Deutschland ein fußballbegeistertes Land ist. Die verbindende Kraft unseres Sports ist in diesem Sommer seit dem ersten Turniertag überall zu spüren. In den Stadien und auf den Fanmeilen sind sich Fans aus aller Welt begegnet und haben friedlich gemeinsam den Fußball gefeiert. Wir haben beeindruckende Fanmärsche und in den Host-Cities eine fröhliche und ausgelassene Stimmung erlebt. Und auch vor den Bildschirmen haben Millionen von Menschen Tag für Tag zusammen mit ihren Teams gefiebert, gejubelt und auch gelitten. Das ist Fußball.

Die UEFA EURO 2024 wird auch über das Finale hinaus langfristig wirken. Nicht nur, weil hochklassige Spiele und eine einzigartige Stimmung schon jetzt für bleibende Erinnerungen gesorgt haben. Die EURO hat darüber hinaus auch beim Thema Nachhaltigkeit klare Akzente gesetzt und wird den Amateurfußball durch verschiedene Maßnahmen und Projekte voranbringen. Ich wünsche Ihnen und uns allen fantastische Halbfinalpartien mit begeisterndem Fußball und inspirierenden Begegnungen im und außerhalb des Stadions.

UEFA
EURO 2024
GERMANY

CONTENTS

89

60

TOP SCORERS
– EURO BY EURO

80

SEMI-FINAL CITIES:
MUNICH AND DORTMUND

68

A PARTY IN GERMANY:
THE PICTURES THAT PROVE IT

89

SHOOT-OUT SHOWDOWNS:
PENALTIES OF THE PAST

EDITORIAL
Editor: Roy Gilfoyle
Lead designer: Adam Ward
Designer: Neil Haines
Sub editors: Simon Monk,
Adam Oldfield, Peter Leathley,
Peter Milby, Adrian Caffery,
Scott Squires, Jonah Webb

FOR UEFA
Sam Adams, Emmanuel
Deconche, Christophe Burri,
Lars Bretscher, James Raybaudo,
Thomas Sauvage, Jim Agnew,
Andrin Cooper, Peter Dennis,
Stephen Mines, Dominique Maurer,
Arona Gaye

REACH SPORT
Content sales director:
Fergus McKenna
Head of commercial
partnerships:
David Scripps
Commissioning editor:
Chris Brereton
Operations manager:
Nick Moreton
Marketing & communications
manager:
Claire Brown

PHOTOGRAPHY
UEFA, Alamy

**OFFICIAL LICENSED
PRODUCT
PUBLISHED BY**
Reach Sport

PRINTED BY
Walstead

**A TOBACCO-FREE
TOURNAMENT**
A no-smoking policy is in operation
at UEFA EURO 2024. Thank you for
respecting the no-smoking policy
and enjoy the games.

FULL OF EURO SPIRIT

Spain and Croatia fans have an impromptu kick about in Berlin – another example of the power of football in bringing people of all nations together.

RONALD KOEMAN

A SEMI-FINAL GOALSCORER IN 1988, THE DUTCH LEGEND LOOKS BACK AT THE STAR-STUDDED SIDE THAT WON THAT EURO, ASSESSES WHY IT'S BEEN THE NETHERLANDS' ONLY MAJOR TOURNAMENT VICTORY SO FAR, AND TELLS US ABOUT HIS TWO SPELLS AS NATIONAL TEAM COACH

The last time Germany hosted a EURO, in 1988, was a significant tournament for you and the Netherlands. What was it like to win?

"Yeah, great. It's unique because the Netherlands has only won one tournament, unfortunately. Of course it was great. Firstly, because it was hosted in our neighbouring country as this one is. It helped that we had lots of our fans there to support us.

"The matches felt like home matches. Everybody was very positive. Everybody had the idea we could go a long way in the tournament. At the end we won matches, sometimes with a bit of luck, but that's all in the game, otherwise you can't win. It was magnificent.

Taking the game to the next level.

Atos will support UEFA EURO 2024™ in being the most advanced, widely shared, inclusive, and connected football tournament ever.

Let's move things forward together.
#AdvancingWhatMatters

UEFA EURO 2024 GERMANY

Atos

OFFICIAL IT PARTNER OF UEFA EURO 2024™

"At the time I was a player at PSV Eindhoven. We won the championship, the cup and also the European Cup in 1988. The EURO was like a dessert. So, winning the EURO was a nice experience for the whole country. To see the joy of the supporters when we brought the trophy home was a tremendously nice experience."

Rinus Michels was the coach and you had players in your team like Marco van Basten, Ruud Gullit, Gerald Vanenburg, Frank Rijkaard. Would you say that the team of 1988 was a total football team?
"Well, you could say so. The squad that went to the tournament was put together very well. There was a hierarchy and there were different ages represented within the squad. We also had some top players: Van Basten, Gullit, Rijkaard. It was a good unit with a very experienced coach, Michels.

"During that period he was like a father figure for us. We clicked with each other and we respected him, but it was also the other way around towards the players.

"The relationships within the group were good. The substitutes were also part of the group and they experienced everything. It was all about the 'we' feeling. Nobody thought that their personal interests were more important than the interests of the group. Then you grow in a tournament.

"We played a wonderful game against Germany in the semi-finals, which at the time was a stronger love-hate relationship than it is nowadays, and which eventually ended up with us winning the final.

"As a football player you experience tournaments and periods where everything is okay. Maybe it wasn't the classic Dutch football style. We actually played a 4-4-2 system. That isn't the Dutch school, which should be 4-3-3. It was just well organised."

In the 1988 Ballon d'Or top five were yourself, Van Basten, Gullit, Rijkaard and [Oleksiy] Mykhaylychenko. Is that one of the reasons why this team was that dominant?
"Of course. We were at an age of 25-26 years old. It was an experienced team, but also with younger and older guys like Adri van Tiggelen, Arnold Mühren, my brother Erwin. There was a good mix. And with offensive players like Gullit and Van Basten we had players who made the difference at that tournament."

"During that period he [Michels] was like a father figure for us. We clicked with each other and we respected him, but it was also the other way around towards the players"

→

"You need a trainer who allows you to play in such a way that you can show that you are a good footballer"

You are often described as the ultimate defender, but you also scored more than 200 goals during your career. How would you describe yourself as a player?
"I wasn't a real defender. When I was a younger player, I was a midfielder who ended up in the defence. My strongest points were playing the ball and building up the game. I also had a good awareness.

"I had a great pass, short, long. Of course, I could shoot really well from distance. I practised my free-kicks a lot, so I was also the type of player who had a lot of success in set-piece situations.

"Tactically, I was good as a player, and as a defender I knew what the problems for me were. I didn't want to expose myself to one-on-one sprints against a fast striker and that did happen on occasion and so you would see what my weakness was as a player.

"I was lucky with all of the trainers I have had, such as

Guus Hiddink, Johan Cruyff, who always gave me, certainly as a central defender, the freedom to move up into midfield and further up the pitch from where I could take shots and score goals. That is a way of working together. You need a trainer who allows you to play in such a way that you can show that you are a good footballer."

Does the Ronald Koeman type of player exist these days?
"No, not really any more. Actually, in today's football, often the central defender thinks defensively, looks after how the defence is set up.

"Nowadays, the left-backs and right-backs are often wingers. What I did from the middle of the defence is now being done from the flanks or from the left-back or right-back positions and not so much from the centre of defence.

"There are now more defenders whose strength lies in defending well and being physically strong. My strong point was to play a more attacking role, coming out of defence, and that is something you don't really see any more."

You mentioned earlier that 1988 was the year the Netherlands won their only international trophy. How much does that surprise you?
"Perhaps it can be explained by the fact that we are not the biggest country. We do not have a large pool of players to choose from, but we always produce good, young players, players who develop themselves quite well in the Netherlands which means that we are always going to be a country that only just wins or only just loses.

"We have, of course, played a number of finals that we have unfortunately lost. So I think that what the Netherlands as a nation has done in the last 40, 50 years is really quite good. But yes, countries such as Germany, Brazil, Spain, have many more footballers than we do in the Netherlands. Those sorts of countries are a little bit ahead of us.

"But the Netherlands is a country that can compete and also has a chance. It has not always been successful but that is also what sport is about."

You have had two spells in charge of your national team. First time around you reached the final of the UEFA Nations League. How do you look back at that time?
"It was a really nice period because from the moment I became coach of the national team, there was a lot of criticism of the Dutch side. It was seen as not being any good, it also wasn't good to watch. There was also the idea that the connection to the players was not what it perhaps is nowadays. We are with each other now.

"We have started something and we have talked about that with each other. We have to have a bit of pride, you have to have that if you are selected. You have to show that you are happy and available to play for the national team. That side of things improved, as did the results and we qualified for the finals of a tournament.

"So that is something that has developed and the performances were good. In the end we made it into the final of the UEFA Nations League and people started to like the national team more than was the case in the period before."

➤

What has your second spell as national team coach been like?

"In principle we still have a strong squad now. I think that we have been a little unlucky with quite a few injuries during the past year and also for sure a lot of injuries to players who were more than valuable for the national team. The players are five years older of course than in my first period and we are seeing younger players coming through again.

"Xavi Simons, Tijjani Reijnders, [Lutsharel] Geertruida, [Quilindschy] Hartman, [Mats] Wieffer, [Jerdy] Schouten, [Joey] Veerman, you name it. Many of these guys play in the Netherlands and have developed into national team players.

"The current group is a very good one. I think many countries are envious of the number of central defenders we have in our squad. They all play for big clubs and it is a difficult choice for me to pick the best players.

"We feel we still have a lot of quality in this squad."

Is there a parallel between the team of 1988 and the current squad, with so many Dutch players currently with Italian clubs?

"I don't know about parallels. In our time, 1988, they were attackers. Players who made the difference like Gullit, with his attacking qualities, Van Basten, a technical number nine with great efficiency in front of goal.

"The guys who play there now are midfielders and defenders. Maybe we have developed more central defenders, wing-backs and midfielders and perhaps not enough attackers.

"We have fewer options in attack than at the back."

> **"He [Simons] is developing incredibly well. Sometimes we want too much, too soon of these young players. You have to give them time, also within the Dutch national team"**

One player around the current squad that excites supporters is Xavi Simons. How do you rate his progress?

"Well, he is a big talent who makes conscious choices about where he will play. He made a deliberate choice to go from Paris St-Germain to PSV. Then moving on to Leipzig in the Bundesliga.

"He is developing incredibly well. Sometimes we want too much, too soon of these young players. You have to give them time, also within the Dutch national team. It is different from playing at your club. But those are the types of players who will become big stars as they have so much quality.

"He has played at the highest level from a young age. He has played against [Real] Madrid in the [UEFA] Champions League. It is wonderful that he has all these experiences already."

QUARTER-FINAL ACTION

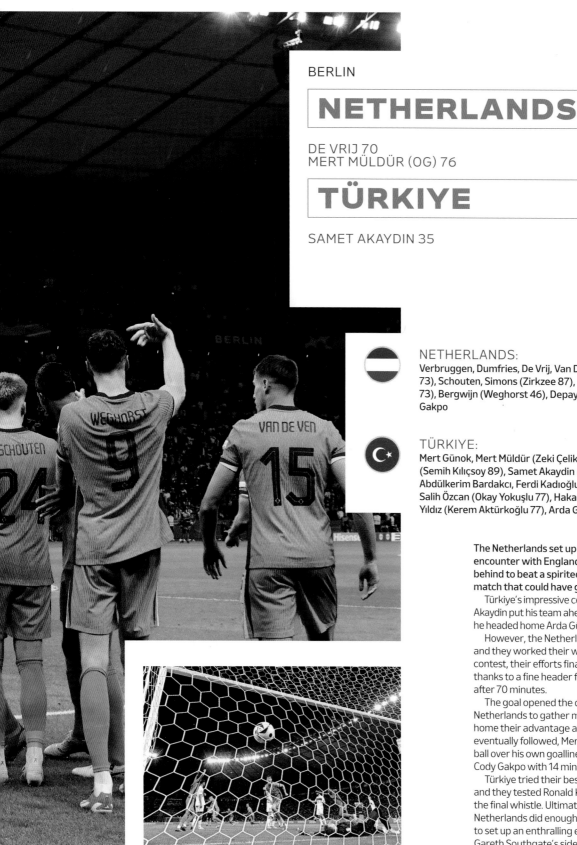

BERLIN

NETHERLANDS 2

DE VRIJ 70
MERT MÜLDÜR (OG) 76

TÜRKIYE 1

SAMET AKAYDIN 35

NETHERLANDS:
Verbruggen, Dumfries, De Vrij, Van Dijk, Aké (Van de Ven 73), Schouten, Simons (Zirkzee 87), Reijnders (Veerman 73), Bergwijn (Weghorst 46), Depay (Frimpong 87), Gakpo

TÜRKIYE:
Mert Günok, Mert Müldür (Zeki Çelik 82), Kaan Ayhan (Semih Kılıçsoy 89), Samet Akaydin (Cenk Tosun 82), Abdülkerim Bardakcı, Ferdi Kadıoğlu, Barış Alper Yılmaz, Salih Özcan (Okay Yokuşlu 77), Hakan Çalhanoğlu, Kenan Yıldız (Kerem Aktürkoğlu 77), Arda Güler

The Netherlands set up a semi-final encounter with England as they came from behind to beat a spirited Türkiye side in a match that could have gone either way.

Türkiye's impressive central defender Samet Akaydin put his team ahead after 35 minutes as he headed home Arda Güler's cross.

However, the Netherlands refused to panic and they worked their way back into the contest, their efforts finally being rewarded thanks to a fine header from Stefan de Vrij after 70 minutes.

The goal opened the door for the Netherlands to gather momentum and press home their advantage and an own goal eventually followed, Mert Müldür bundling the ball over his own goalline under pressure from Cody Gakpo with 14 minutes remaining.

Türkiye tried their best to find an equaliser and they tested Ronald Koeman's men to the final whistle. Ultimately though, the Netherlands did enough to hold on for the win to set up an enthralling encounter against Gareth Southgate's side.

"You see how everyone reacts and works together. We did everything we could, with tackles and saves. Now it's time to recover and prepare for another tough match"

———————— Virgil van Dijk

"We had to show our mentality. To be 1-0 down against this team who are very, very strong defensively, who work so hard with all the fans behind them... that's a good side to show"

——————— Nathan Aké

"For the whole nation it's something special. We're a small nation and we're in the semi-finals with England, France and Spain. We are really proud"

——————— Ronald Koeman

GROUP STAGE

MATCH 1

POLAND **1** v **2** NETHERLANDS

Buksa 16   Gakpo 29,
Weghorst 83

MATCH 2

NETHERLANDS **0** v **0** FRANCE

MATCH 3

NETHERLANDS **2** v **3** AUSTRIA

Gakpo 47,   Malen (og) 6,
Depay 75   Schmid 59,
      Sabitzer 80

ROUND OF 16

ROMANIA **0** v **3** NETHERLANDS

Gakpo 20,
Malen 83, 90+3

QUARTER-FINALS

NETHERLANDS **2** v **1** TÜRKIYE

De Vrij 70,   Akaydin 35
M. Müldür (og) 76

ROAD TO THE SEMI-FINALS
ENGLAND

GROUP STAGE

MATCH 1

SERBIA **0** v **1** ENGLAND

Bellingham 13

MATCH 2

DENMARK **1** v **1** ENGLAND

Hjulmand 34   Kane 18

MATCH 3

ENGLAND **0** v **0** SLOVENIA

ROUND OF 16

ENGLAND **2** v **1** SLOVAKIA

Bellingham 90+5,   Schranz 25
Kane 91

After extra time

QUARTER-FINALS

ENGLAND **1** v **1** SWITZERLAND

Saka 80   Embolo 75

England win 5-3 on penalties

QUARTER-FINAL ACTION

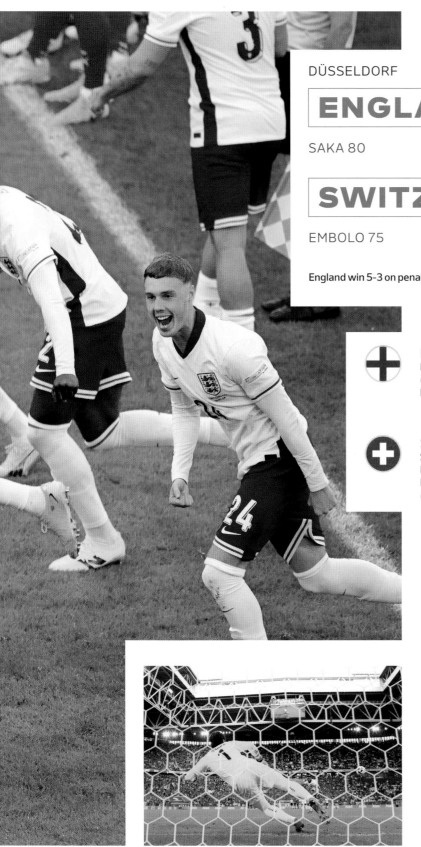

DÜSSELDORF

ENGLAND 1

SAKA 80

SWITZERLAND 1

EMBOLO 75

England win 5-3 on penalties

ENGLAND:
Pickford, Walker, Konsa (Palmer 78), Stones, Trippier (Eze 78), Mainoo (Shaw 78), Rice, Saka, Bellingham, Foden (Alexander-Arnold 115), Kane (Toney 110)

SWITZERLAND:
Sommer, Schär, Akanji, Rodríguez, Rieder (Zuber 63), Freuler (Sierro 118), Xhaka, Aebischer (Amdouni 118), Ndoye (Zakaria 98), Embolo (Shaqiri 109), Vargas (Widmer 63)

England had Jordan Pickford and five decisive penalty-takers to thank as the Three Lions did just enough to make the UEFA EURO 2024 semi-finals after a nail-biting shoot-out victory against a determined Switzerland outfit who will feel unlucky to go home empty handed.

Trent Alexander-Arnold scored the decisive penalty to seal the victory for England after Pickford had given his side the advantage by saving Manuel Akanji's effort.

Earlier, Breel Embolo had opened the scoring for Switzerland after 75 minutes as he converted a cross that bobbled across the box but England found another gear thanks to Bukayo Saka's stunning left-footed equaliser five minutes later.

There was nothing between the sides in extra time and when it came to the penalty shoot-out, England looked in decisive form, converting every effort as they booked their spot in the last four.

It was a challenging evening for Gareth Southgate's men but they remain on course for a second successive EURO final.

"The pressure [of taking penalties] is something I embrace. You fail once but I'm the sort of guy who wants to put myself in the position again. I kept my cool and scored my penalty"

—————— Bukayo Saka

"We knew it was going to be tight, we were never going to run away with the game although that would have been nice"

———— Trent Alexander-Arnold

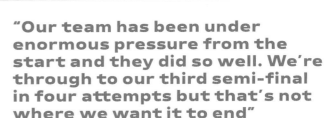

"Our team has been under enormous pressure from the start and they did so well. We're through to our third semi-final in four attempts but that's not where we want it to end"

———— Gareth Southgate

NETHERLANDS

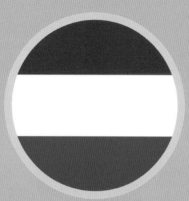

Momentum is often cited as a crucial factor in helping a group of players win an international football tournament and the Netherlands can confidently suggest that they have that asset in abundance at the moment.

When you take a look at the last four teams at UEFA EURO 2024, the Netherlands are the only side that did not require at least extra time to book their spot in the semi-finals.

Indeed, tonight's opposition, England, and France, both required a penalty shoot-out to get this far.

Yet the Netherlands also know all about having to dig deep – and they know it is a virtue that can take a team very far indeed.

They were written off in some quarters after a 3-2 group-stage defeat by Austria meant they only qualified for the round of 16 as one of the best third-placed teams.

Since then though, a fine 3-0 win over Romania and a brilliant comeback victory against Türkiye has earned them a spot in tonight's semi-final with England.

Ronald Koeman's side may have taken a circuitous route to this stage of the tournament but he has a dressing room crammed full of talent, dedication and experience.

Players such as Bart Verbruggen, Cody Gakpo, Virgil van Dijk, Stefan de Vrij and Tijjani Reijnders have all proven their worth before in a Netherlands shirt and although England provide a formidable test, Koeman's team will hope they are building up a head of steam at just the right time.

> "We are in the semi-finals of the European Championship – nobody expected that. If all goes well, we will play two more games"
>
> — **Ronald Koeman**

EURO RECORD

1960	Did not enter
1964	Did not qualify
1968	Did not qualify
1972	Did not qualify
1976	Third place
1980	Group stage
1984	Did not qualify
1988	Winners
1992	Semi-finals
1996	Quarter-finals
2000	Semi-finals
2004	Semi-finals
2008	Quarter-finals
2012	Group stage
2016	Did not qualify
2020	Round of 16

TOP GOALSCORER

This tournament

CODY GAKPO

3

THE COACH
RONALD KOEMAN

As a much-revered and decorated player in the 1980s and 1990s, few footballers in Europe were as good as Ronald Koeman.

And the Dutchman now has the chance to underline his international pedigree in the dugout as well. After nearly two decades in the domestic game, managing teams such as Ajax, Benfica, PSV, Valencia, Southampton and Everton, this is the perfect chance for Koeman to show that he can take his nation all the way.

Of course, this is not Koeman's first spell in charge of the Netherlands, having helped them qualify for UEFA EURO 2020. He left his position to take on the top job at Barcelona but following Louis van Gaal's retirement as Netherlands boss, Koeman was reinstalled as head coach in January 2023 – and they have not looked back since.

As a player, Koeman was renowned for his immense fitness, dedication, ability on the ball but also, just as crucially, his all-round footballing intelligence.

He has clearly instilled these qualities in his players to good effect. Koeman is a head coach who expects – and deserves – ultimate respect and devotion from his squad and the way the Netherlands have played so far in this tournament proves that he has achieved that goal with aplomb.

PLAYER FOCUS

CODY GAKPO

No team gets to the semi-final of a UEFA European Championship thanks to the virtues and abilites of one player alone but Cody Gakpo's efforts in Germany have shown both his fellow squad members and the footballing world that he is a truly vital cog in the Netherlands' machine at this tournament.

Gakpo has been a constant thorn in the side of the opposition during EURO 2024 and all the signs are there that he is not finished yet.

The Liverpool forward can be employed across the entire frontline but it is his ability to cut back inside off his preferred left wing that allows him to create chances.

His eye for goal, combined with a brilliant work ethic and stamina rate, mark him out as a player who never gives in – and who always knows how to cause maximum damage.

STATS

3 GOALS

1 ASSIST

NATHAN AKÉ

Nathan Aké knows all about being a crucial part of a successful fooballing outfit thanks to his time at Manchester City and he is demonstrating the same qualities here again in Germany.

There are few better and more effective defenders at this tournament than the 29-year-old.

His ability in the centre of defence offers comfort and support to both his goalkeeper behind him and the players in front, and he is equally comfortable at full-back.

He has played 384 minutes so far at UEFA EURO 2024 and has helped ensure that the Netherlands' defence is one of the most miserly in the tournament. As well as his solidity at the back, Aké also offers plenty of aerial threat going forward and his experience at the highest levels of the domestic game are coming to the fore in Germany.

STATS

7 TACKLES

21 BALLS RECOVERED

XAVI SIMONS

When Xavi Simons arrived at UEFA EURO 2024, he was widely deemed to be a star of the future.

Forget that. He is a star now. The 21-year-old attacking midfielder has grown into one of the Bundesliga's most impressive players – and he has only underlined that even further during this tournament.

His rise to prominence in a Netherlands shirt has been swift, dramatic and although he rarely featured in the 2022 FIFA World Cup in Qatar he has now become a huge part of Ronald Koeman's plans.

Koeman has entrusted Simons with the task of causing opposition defenders maximum trouble and his explosive pace, dribbling ability and threat in front of goal have more than repaid his head coach's trust. Dutch fans will hope to see these qualities on show again tonight.

STATS

2 ASSISTS

367 MINUTES PLAYED

X100 Series 5G

Co-engineered with ZEISS

Photography. Redefined.

ENGLAND

Could England's long, long wait for international glory be about to end?

Three Lions fans follow their team around the world in the hope that one day they can once again celebrate in the same manner as they last did on the international stage, an astonishing 58 years ago.

That is how long is has been since England fans and players last tasted serious international success, when their much-revered team at the 1966 FIFA World Cup brought home the Jules Rimet Trophy.

Three years ago in the final of UEFA EURO 2020, England were one match away from ending that hiatus but they fell just short, their home fans at Wembley Stadium left heartbroken by Italy's nerveless penalty shoot-out victory.

But Gareth Southgate's men have shrugged that disappointment off and appear to be heading in the right direction once again.

England looked disjointed in the group stages yet came through unscathed and knockout wins against Slovakia and Switzerland have helped the team to build up some priceless momentum.

Southgate has a truly incredible set of players at his disposal with the likes of Phil Foden, Kyle Walker, Harry Kane and Jude Bellingham among the very best in the world.

At UEFA EURO 2020 they played a brand of fast-paced and fearless football that they have not quite managed to emulate in Germany.

Yet they are still here, still striving for glory. They have come this far – but how much further can they go?

"I thought the players were brilliant [against Switzerland]. It's the best we've played. We caused them a lot of problems"

Gareth Southgate

EURO RECORD

1960	Did not enter
1964	Did not qualify
1968	Third place
1972	Did not qualify
1976	Did not qualify
1980	Group stage
1984	Did not qualify
1988	Group stage
1992	Group stage
1996	Semi-finals
2000	Group stage
2004	Quarter-finals
2008	Did not qualify
2012	Quarter-finals
2016	Round of 16
2020	Runners-up

TOP GOALSCORERS

This tournament

JUDE BELLINGHAM/ HARRY KANE

2

THE COACH
GARETH SOUTHGATE

Few head coaches at UEFA EURO 2024 have been under as much pressure as England manager Gareth Southgate.

Even fewer can say they know precisely what their players are going through on the pitch, when the pressure is at its absolute highest.

Famously, Southgate missed a pivotal penalty shoot-out effort for the Three Lions against Germany at EURO '96, which eventually saw England lose at Wembley.

Three years ago, with Southgate now in charge of England, history repeated itself as his side again suffered EURO penalty heartbreak in the same stadium, losing in the final to Italy.

Yet Southgate's undoubted human qualities – and his ability to absorb the pressure that comes as part and parcel of being England's manager – means that his squad at EURO 2024 looks as committed and as eager as ever to help England lift their first piece of major silverware in nearly six decades.

As well as narrowly missing out on EURO glory, Southgate guided England to the semi-finals of the 2018 FIFA World Cup and he is a man who has managed to take England closer than ever to international glory. He knows though that his work is not done as another huge challenge awaits tonight.

PLAYER FOCUS

JUDE BELLINGHAM

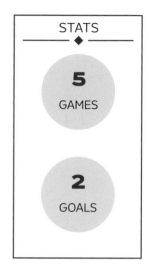

The more pressure put on the shoulders of Jude Bellingham, the better he seems to get.

After a truly sensational season with Real Madrid, where he proved that he was scared of no side, no club and, as importantly no expectation placed on his young shoulders, Bellingham has been one of England's most pivotal and decisive performers at UEFA EURO 2024.

In England's first group match against Serbia, he scored the only goal of the game to get the Three Lions up and running and then his overhead kick equaliser against Slovakia in the round of 16 was arguably the goal of the tournament.

Bellingham is just 21 but he plays with the maturity, vision and excellence of a player many years older. England have a true gem in Bellingham.

STATS

5 GAMES

2 GOALS

DECLAN RICE

Every successful international football team in the history of the game has understood one thing: not every outfield player can steal the headlines.

And in Declan Rice, England have a player who understands that more than most.

The Arsenal midfielder is a bona fide footballing superstar – but he would be the last man to tell you so.

In an England jersey he is surrounded by box-office names and talent and while he also deserves his place among the highest-calibre players in Europe, the England midfielder never lets it show.

At UEFA EURO 2024 he has again displayed his selfless virtues. His his hard work, understanding of the game and ability to both stop and start offensive moves mark him out as a player destined for true greatness.

STATS

5 GAMES

510 MINUTES PLAYED

BUKAYO SAKA

For a 22-year-old who is still learning his job, Bukayo Saka already knows plenty about the highs and lows that international football can bring.

It was Saka, still a teenager, who missed England's last – and crucial – penalty against Italy in the final of UEFA EURO 2020 and that heartbreak and disappointment could well have led to him removing himself from the limelight and affecting his pure enthusiasm for the game.

Instead, the Arsenal star has been sensational at EURO 2024, proving any doubters wrong and showing why Gareth Southgate has such faith in him. His equalising goal last weekend against Switzerland underlined his attacking abilities while his penalty shoot-out success demonstrated his courage and character. Saka is clearly loving his time in Germany – and the best might still be to come.

STATS

5 GAMES

50.4km DISTANCE COVERED

75 Jahre Grundgesetz

„AUCH DIE DIGITALE WÜRDE DES MENSCHEN IST UNANTASTBAR."

Lasst uns gemeinsam die Demokratie im Netz stärken.
Werde Teil der Telekom Initiative „Gegen Hass im Netz".

Gemeinsam #GegenHassImNetz

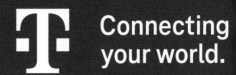

MEET THE MASCOT:
ALBÄRT

One of the most instantly recognisable figures at this summer's tournament is Albärt: the official mascot for UEFA EURO 2024.

Given his name in a vote by children in UEFA's Football in Schools programme along with fans on UEFA.com, Albärt fought off competition from other bear-related shortlisted names such as Bärnardo, Bärnheart and Herzi von Bär.

The EURO mascot pays homage to the popular children's teddy bear toy, which is said to have originated in Germany in the early 20th century.

Albärt's debut was at a friendly match in Gelsenkirchen where the national team faced Colombia. However, his first public appearance was earlier that day at a local primary school, showcasing his commitment to stirring up excitement about football among children across Europe.

He has continued to visit schools across Europe and also joined forces with Germany's football star Jamal Musiala,

taking on the role of 'Substitute Teacher' in a series of EURO-themed lessons and challenges. These initiatives are designed to motivate children to be active and #MakeMoves including encouraging them to invent unique skills and celebrations, which can be transformed into mascot animations using motion-capture technology.

Further extending his reach, Albärt has ventured into the virtual world with his own island in the popular Roblox game, Piñata Smashlings™. Here, he continues to engage young fans in their digital playground, inspiring them to carry their virtual activities into the real world to stay active and healthy.

Albärt has had a busy tournament, touring the host cities throughout Germany, meeting fans and supporting the teams. His mission is ambitious: to inspire ten million children across Europe to get active, as he follows in the iconic, oversized footsteps of previous mascots like Berni, Goaliath, Rabbit, and Kinas.

MOMENTS WORTH
STOPPING FOR

INDONESIA

QATAR

BOOK YOUR QATAR
STOPOVER NOW
FROM 14$*

*Terms and conditions apply

visit
QATAR

FUSSBALLLIEBE FINALE TAKES CENTRE STAGE

The tournament's official match ball has been given a fresh new look for the UEFA EURO 2024 semi-finals and final.

adidas has produced a bespoke match ball for the UEFA EURO 2024 semi-finals and final: the FUSSBALLLIEBE FINALE.

The official match ball that the four remaining teams going for glory will use sees a refresh of the iconic visual elements from the ball that kicked things off back on 14 June. The prominent black wing shapes have been accentuated with vibrant edges, curves and dots that take on the unmistakable black, red and gold of the host nation, Germany.

The white base is replaced with an eye-catching silver, representing the silverware that the final four teams will be competing for. The silver colour of the ball has been specially developed and tested with athletes to ensure that it stands out on the pitch without reflecting light back off the surface.

It will be the first ball used in a EURO final to feature Connected Ball technology – which delivers precise ball data to video match officials in real time. Combining player position data with AI, the innovation contributes to UEFA's semi-automated offside technology and has been key to supporting in-match decisions throughout the tournament.

The technology also enhances the overall fan viewing experience by offering accurate measurement of in-play data – including the ball speed, spin and distance the ball travelled before hitting the back of the net to watching fans.

The ball's CTR-CORE is designed for accuracy and consistency, promoting fast, precise play with maximum shape and air retention. The PRECISIONSHELL polyurethane (PU) skin features micro and macro textures and a 20-piece panel shape designed for enhanced aerodynamics.

As well as using recycled polyester and water-based ink, FUSSBALLLIEBE FINALE is made from more sustainable bio-based materials than any previous adidas official match ball. Every layer of the ball has been adjusted to include materials such as corn fibres, sugar cane, wood pulp and rubber.

FIRE IS SONG OF SUMMER

Italian electronic trio MEDUZA, GRAMMY® nominated OneRepublic, and German singer-songwriter Leony are the big names behind the official UEFA EURO 2024 song, called FIRE.

The song sits alongside the #LightYourFire campaign which invites fans globally to share their passion.

The three acts have brought their own touch to the track – and their own take on what it means to them: for MEDUZA, the song merges their love for football with their music, emphasising the unifying power of music amidst excitement for the tournament; OneRepublic's Ryan Tedder sees the song as an inspiration to unite fans worldwide; this echoes Leony's childhood love for football and her joy in contributing to the official tournament song.

'FIRE' embodies the spirit of football and music enthusiasts, blending MEDUZA's anthemic house production, OneRepublic's compelling soundscapes, and Leony's pop expertise into a celebration of unity and exhilaration. It serves as a timeless soundtrack for UEFA EURO 2024.

The artists perform the anthem live at the closing ceremony just before kick-off, adding to the event's finale. Additionally, MEDUZA have also created a full auditory experience, a series of compositions inspired by the anthem to enrich TV sequences, walk-on music for teams entering the pitch, and key moments like the trophy presentation, ensuring that the spirit of UEFA EURO 2024 resonates in every aspect of the event, uniting music and football.

An official playlist is available on streaming platforms, providing a backdrop to the tournament.

MUNICH FOOTBALL ARENA

MUNICH FOOTBALL ARENA

CAPACITY:
66,000

HOME TO:
BAYERN MÜNCHEN

UEFA EURO 2024 CITY AMBASSADOR:
DR FELIX BRYCH

MUNICH MUNICH MUNICH MUNICH

ONE OF THE CONTINENT'S MOST ICONIC STADIUMS ADDS ANOTHER BIG MATCH TO AN ALREADY IMPRESSIVE CV

There can't be many more recognisable stadiums in world football than the Munich Football Arena – and it's ready to be the focus of global attention once again.

It may be less than 20 years since the venue first opened its doors to the world but it has already played host to many mammoth events and memorable matches, including some during UEFA EURO 2020 and the 2006 FIFA World Cup.

Its stunning colour-changing exterior makes it one of the most iconic stadiums around – but the most important thing to fans of Bayern München is that they can call this fantastic place home.

Bayern's previous base was Munich's Olympic Stadium, which they shared with 1860 München. By the tail end of the last century fans of both clubs were keen to play at a purpose-built football stadium and options were explored.

While the city's political leaders favoured redevelopment of the Olympic Stadium, the clubs were adamant that a new ground would bring greater benefits and a site in Fröttmaning was identified.

A referendum of the citizens of Munich confirmed that the public were behind the move and by 2002 the foundation stone had been laid and construction began.

While the building was going on, it was announced that the new stadium would host six matches at the 2006 FIFA World Cup and by April 2005 lead construction company

Alpine Bau had finished their work.

The following month, both home teams played their inaugural matches at the official opening, 1860 taking on Nürnberg while Bayern played against the Germany national team in front of sell-out 66,000 crowds.

Fans witnessed the first Bundesliga match at the stadium when Bayern beat Borussia Mönchengladbach 3-0 in the opening game of the 2005/06 season – and by the end of the campaign the club were celebrating a league and cup double.

Meanwhile, Bayern bought out 1860 München's share of the stadium to become the sole owners, though 1860 would still play their home matches at the Munich Football Arena until 2017.

In 2006, the eyes of the world were on this spectacular new stadium as it hosted the opening match of the World Cup when local hero Philipp Lahm got the party started in Germany's 4-2 win against Costa Rica. Five more matches would be staged there including a semi-final.

The next major occasion to draw a massive global audience came in 2012 when there was again plenty of local interest as Bayern took on Chelsea in the UEFA Champions League final. While the event was stunning, the result didn't go the way home fans would have liked – though there's always the chance for redemption when the final returns to Munich in 2025.

There's never a chance to rest on laurels

in the pursuit of excellence and since it was opened there have been adjustments to the stadium.

In 2012, the Bayern München Museum was opened, the biggest club museum in Germany, while the departure of 1860 in 2017 meant Bayern fans could make the stadium feel even more like home as the club made a greater number of the seats in the ground red, incorporating the club motto and crest into the stands. Around the same time, the largest video walls in any European stadium were installed, along with improved floodlights that are brighter and able to change colour.

In 2021 the delayed UEFA EURO 2020 bandwagon rolled into town and the Munich Football Arena hosted four matches, including all of Germany's group games, though attendances were reduced as the effects of the COVID-19 pandemic continued to be felt.

Interestingly, the Arena makes history this year by becoming the first venue to host matches in consecutive EUROs.

While football is its bread and butter, the first big non-football event took place in 2022 when an NFL International Series match between the Seattle Seahawks and Tampa Bay Buccaneers took place, while the doors are also open for large-scale concerts.

Football will always be the heart and soul of the Munich Football Arena, where Bayern have already celebrated 14 Bundesliga title wins, and football will be the only thing on the minds of the fans right now.

WHEN THE EYES OF THE FOOTBALL WORLD WERE ON MUNICH FOOTBALL ARENA...

2006 FIFA WORLD CUP

Six drama-filled matches took place at Football Arena Munich, where fans got to see the home nation perform twice.

An opening match between Germany and Costa Rica containing six goals set the tone, a match topped and tailed by stunning strikes from Philipp Lahm and Torsten Frings.

Holders Brazil cruised through their match with Australia, Tunisia and Saudi Arabia shared four goals, while the Ivory Coast turned a two-goal deficit into a 3-2 win against Serbia and Montenegro.

The hosts ousted Sweden in the round of 16 and the last match in Munich was the semi-final that saw France progress to the final at Portugal's expense.

◆

GERMANY 4 v 2 COSTA RICA
(GROUP MATCH)

TUNISIA 2 v 2 SAUDI ARABIA
(GROUP MATCH)

BRAZIL 2 v 0 AUSTRALIA
(GROUP MATCH)

IVORY COAST 3 v 2 SERBIA AND MONTENEGRO
(GROUP MATCH)

GERMANY 2 v 0 SWEDEN
(ROUND OF 16)

PORTUGAL 0 v 1 FRANCE
(SEMI-FINAL)

2012 UEFA CHAMPIONS LEAGUE FINAL

Thomas Müller must have thought his goal had won the European Cup for Bayern München when he struck in the 83rd minute against Chelsea in the continent's biggest club match of the year.

Didier Drogba had other ideas and equalised five minutes later to take the game to extra time, but a winning goal evaded both teams.

A penalty shoot-out was needed and even though Juan Mata missed the first for the English side, they converted the rest to win 4-3.

◆

| BAYERN MÜNCHEN | 1 v 1 | CHELSEA |

(CHELSEA WON 4-3 ON PENALTIES)

UEFA EURO 2020

It was a mixed bag for the home team as Germany won, drew and lost group games in Munich but progressed to the knockout rounds.

A defeat by France was followed by an eventful 4-2 win over holders Portugal and a draw with Hungary in which they had to recover from deficits twice to finish 2-2.

Eventual champions Italy stopped off in Munich en route to the final, beating Belgium 2-1 at the quarter-final stage.

◆

| FRANCE | 1 v 0 | GERMANY |
(GROUP MATCH)

| PORTUGAL | 2 v 4 | GERMANY |
(GROUP MATCH)

| GERMANY | 2 v 2 | HUNGARY |
(GROUP MATCH)

| BELGIUM | 1 v 2 | ITALY |
(QUARTER-FINAL)

DORTMUND
DORTMUND
DORTMUND
DORTMUND
DORTMUND

ONE OF THE WORLD'S GREAT FOOTBALL CATHEDRALS IS READY TO PLAY HOST TO ANOTHER HUGE INTERNATIONAL OCCASION

The 'Yellow Wall' awaits two sets of star players for a UEFA EURO 2024 semi-final and as seen during Borussia Dortmund home games, they can expect an atmosphere as good as any in football.

BVB Stadion Dortmund is the biggest venue at this EURO – though it doesn't have the largest capacity for this tournament – and the huge terrace known locally as 'Die Gelbe Wand' is famed around the footballing world for its colour, passion and noise.

It must be exactly what Dortmund fans had hoped for when the green light was given for a new stadium to be built to allow their club to leave their former Rote Erde home, which still exists and lies adjacent to its considerably larger modern counterpart.

In 1965 it was decided that it was better to create a new stadium rather than try to renovate their former residence but it wasn't until preparations for the 1974 FIFA World Cup started to take shape that momentum could really begin to build.

Cologne pulled out of their bid to host matches at the tournament, allowing Dortmund the opportunity to take their place, and with it the support to plough into creating a venue fit to host matches at the world's biggest football event.

It was not until 1970 that the decision was finally made to begin construction of Dortmund's new Westfalenstadion and on 2 April 1974 the new stadium was unveiled to the public.

The new capacity was 54,000, with a roof that covered the majority of spectators, and a friendly match against Schalke 04 allowed fans to get a taste of what it would be like in their new surroundings.

A few months later the stadium welcomed the Netherlands, Brazil, Sweden, Scotland, Bulgaria and Zaire as it hosted four matches during the World Cup and before long Borussia Dortmund were resuming life in the German second division playing in a stadium that deserved a greater stage. A greater stage is what it got when Dortmund regained their place in the Bundesliga in 1976, though it would be 1995 before they would claim the title for the first time.

By 1992 it was time to upgrade the facilities at the ground still further and phased improvements over the coming decade and in the lead-up to the 2006 World Cup would greatly increase the capacity, including the expansion of the south stand to almost 25,000 to make it the largest stand in Europe.

Early in the 21st century, as part of work to add capacity in the corners of the ground, distinctive giant yellow pylons were added around the outside, enhancing its already-unique identity.

A sign of its growing reputation in Europe, in 2001 the BVB Stadion Dortmund was a major final host as the showpiece event in the UEFA Cup came to North Rhine-Westphalia – and it was a memorable contest too as Liverpool beat Alavés 5-4. It wasn't the first time a major final was staged there though. In the days when the UEFA Cup final was a two-legged affair, Dortmund hosted Juventus in 1993 before the return match in Turin.

Fans at the stadium also saw UEFA Champions League action for the first time during the 1995/96 season and even more vivid memories were made the following season as another run in the continent's most prestigious club competition saw Dortmund go all the way and bring the giant trophy home.

By the time the 2006 World Cup came around, the stadium had reached standards befitting the greatest stage in football competition and six matches were hosted, including the semi-final involving Germany. Italy may have won that day but Dortmund enjoyed contributing to the feelgood factor surrounding German football at the time.

The modernisation work has continued with annual adjustments helping to keep the BVB Stadion Dortmund in the conversation when European fans talk about the best places in the continent to watch football.

Anyone who has taken in the Dortmund experience during the matches staged here at UEFA EURO 2024 can't fail to have been impressed.

BVB
STADION
DORTMUND

**BVB
STADION
DORTMUND**

CAPACITY:
62,000

HOME TO:
BORUSSIA
DORTMUND

**UEFA EURO 2024
CITY AMBASSADORS:**
ROMAN
WEIDENFELLER,
ANNIKE KRAHN

WHEN THE EYES OF THE FOOTBALL WORLD WERE ON BVB STADION DORTMUND...

1974 FIFA WORLD CUP

Johan Cruyff was the star of a multi-talented Netherlands side that played at the BVB Stadion Dortmund three times during this World Cup.

He and Johannes Neeskens scored fantastic goals to see off Brazil in the second group phase and book their place in the final.

The Netherlands had played in Dortmund twice in the first group phase, two penalties from Neeskens doing much of the damage in a 4-1 win against Bulgaria, having already drawn 0-0 with Sweden.

The other match was Scotland's 2-0 win over Zaire, though both teams failed to advance to the second round.

ZAIRE **0** v **2** SCOTLAND
(GROUP STAGE FIRST ROUND)

NETHERLANDS **0** v **0** SWEDEN
(GROUP STAGE FIRST ROUND)

BULGARIA **1** v **4** NETHERLANDS
(GROUP STAGE FIRST ROUND)

NETHERLANDS **2** v **0** BRAZIL
(GROUP STAGE SECOND ROUND)

2001 UEFA CUP FINAL

It took a golden goal to do it, but Liverpool eventually shook off Alavés to win the UEFA Cup for a third time in one of the most compelling European finals ever staged.

The Reds were 2-0 up after 16 minutes and 3-1 ahead at half-time, but the Spanish side replied twice through Javier Moreno straight after half-time.

Robbie Fowler put Liverpool 4-3 up only for Jordi Cruyff to fittingly equalise on the ground his father had graced 27 years earlier.

With just a few minutes to go until penalties were required, the unfortunate Delfi Geli flicked a Gary McAllister free-kick into his own net to settle the outcome.

◆

LIVERPOOL 5 v 4 ALAVÉS

(LIVERPOOL WIN WITH A GOLDEN GOAL)

2006 FIFA WORLD CUP

Anyone who had a ticket for all six matches at BVB Stadion Dortmund during this World Cup would have been able to see home favourites Germany as well as title holders Brazil in action twice each.

The most dramatic match was the group game between Germany and Poland where fans had to wait more than 90 minutes to see the only goal, a late winner from Oliver Neuville.

The next time they would see Jürgen Klinsmann's men in action was the semi-final where Italy triumphed 2-0.

Brazil scored seven goals in their two matches in Dortmund, a 4-1 group win against Japan followed by a 3-0 round-of-16 victory over Ghana.

◆

TRINIDAD AND TOBAGO 0 v 0 SWEDEN

(GROUP MATCH)

GERMANY 1 v 0 POLAND

(GROUP MATCH)

TOGO 0 v 2 SWITZERLAND

(GROUP MATCH)

JAPAN 1 v 4 BRAZIL

(GROUP MATCH)

BRAZIL 3 v 0 GHANA

(ROUND OF 16)

GERMANY 0 v 2 ITALY

(SEMI-FINAL)

MAKE A SAFETY STATEMENT

I DRIVE SLOW

OUSMANE
DEMBELE
FOOTBALLER ICON

United Nations

Supported by **UEFA**

SEMI-FINAL HEROES

THIRTY PLAYERS WHO LED THE CHARGE WHEN A PLACE IN THE FINAL WAS AT STAKE

1960

VALENTIN IVANOV

Two fabulous finishes by Ivanov set the Soviet Union on the road to the final as they overcame Czechoslovakia 3-0 in Marseille.

The number eight was too quick for goalkeeper Viliam Schrojf in slotting in the first before rounding the Czechoslovakian number one to slam in and make it 2-0. Viktor Ponedelnik completed the scoring.

Ivanov ended as joint-top scorer in the inaugural finals and registered four goals at the 1962 FIFA World Cup to finish level with the top scorers there too.

DRAŽAN JERKOVIĆ

The highest-scoring match in EURO history had France leading Yugoslavia 4-2 with 15 minutes to go – and that's as good as it got for the hosts.

Tomislav Knez halved the deficit before Jerković was in the right place at the right time twice in the space of two minutes to turn the match on its head.

Yugoslavia won 5-4 and – just like Ivanov – Jerković was joint-top scorer at both this EURO and the 1962 World Cup.

LUIS SUÁREZ

He might not have got on the scoresheet but Suárez was the man who pulled the strings as Spain overcame a talented Hungary outfit 2-1 after extra time.

Suárez's pass out to the wing began the move that saw Jesús Pereda head in the opener. Though Ferenc Bene equalised and Suárez was carrying an injury for much of the remainder of the match, he was still the man the fans wanted to see on the ball – and Amancio claimed the winner.

Suárez was in the prime of his career at this stage, representing Internazionale where he won Serie A three times and the European Cup twice.

VIKTOR PONEDELNIK

The man who got the winner in the inaugural EURO final four years earlier was at it again as the Soviet Union proved too powerful for Denmark in Barcelona.

Midfielder Valeri Voronin opened the scoring before Ponedelnik put clear daylight between the sides, leaving Valentin Ivanov to complete a 3-0 win.

Ponedelnik's career was defined by his achievements in those first two EUROs and was the last surviving member of the winning 1960 side before his death in 2020.

GIACINTO FACCHETTI

A semi-final that had no goals was dominated by defenders as a strong Soviet Union team were held to a 0-0 draw by an Italian side that played most of the match below strength due to players suffering injuries in the days before substitutes.

Captain Facchetti marshalled his depleted side through a difficult game that ultimately had to be decided by the toss of a coin – and the Internazionale man delighted the home crowd when the right call was made.

Facchetti was a winner at club level as well as international level, winning five Serie A titles and the European Cup twice.

DRAGAN DŽAJIĆ

At a low-scoring EURO, Džajić's two goals were enough to see him finish as top scorer and the first of those decided Yugoslavia's semi-final against England in Florence.

With just a few minutes of the match remaining, Džajić brought the ball down beautifully on his chest before lifting his shot over Gordon Banks. It was a moment of class worthy of winning any match.

He scored in the final too, though Italy prevailed after a replay, and he went on to enjoy a 15-year career in international football.

EVGENI RUDAKOV

The Soviet Union knew they were in for a difficult match when they faced Hungary for a place in the 1972 final and they needed all their defensive resolve.

After Anatoliy Konkov had blasted the USSR into the lead it looked like their hard work would be rewarded, but they needed one more decisive act from goalkeeper Rudakov. With five minutes to go Hungary were awarded a penalty but the keeper guessed the right way to keep Sándor Zámbó's effort out and preserve the 1-0 scoreline.

Though he would lose out in the final, he was named in the Team of the Tournament.

GERD MÜLLER

One of the world's greatest strikers was at his peak during the 1972 UEFA European Championship and two goals from him decided their semi-final against Belgium.

A flicked header put West Germany ahead, then in the second half he got round the back of the Belgian defence to convert coolly.

Odilon Polleunis pulled one back, but West Germany won 2-1 and Müller added two more goals in the 3-0 win over the Soviet Union in the final.

1976

ANTON ONDRUŠ

Czechoslovakia captain Ondruš was a little bit hero and a little bit villain as his team pulled off a remarkable victory over the Netherlands in Zagreb.

In a feisty match that saw three players dismissed, Ondruš scored a fabulous header, then sliced a clearance into his own net as the match went to extra time.

Ondruš – a stylish defender – didn't let his head go down and helped keep Johan Cruyff and his team-mates at bay as two late goals sealed a 3-1 win.

DIETER MÜLLER

When a player scores a hat-trick in a major championship semi-final, it's not difficult to work out who the hero was.

West Germany weren't having it all their own way and found themselves two goals down to Yugoslavia before Heinz Flohe pulled one back, and then another great goalscoring Müller took over.

Only entering the action after coming on as a substitute in the 79th minute, Müller smashed in an equaliser from outside the box a minute later, then scored twice in extra time to settle a 4-2 win.

1984

ANTONIO MACEDA

A goalscoring defender, Maceda was having an eventful time when Spain faced Denmark in their 1984 semi-final.

Maceda's late header against West Germany had sent Spain through at their opponents' expense and his clean strike in the semi-final levelled a match which Spain went on to win on penalties.

Unfortunately, suspension ruled him out of the final, though he did go to the 1986 World Cup two years later as Spain reached the quarter-finals.

JEAN-FRANÇOIS DOMERGUE

The format for the 1980 tournament didn't include semi-finals so four years later it was time for new heroes to emerge.

The 1984 edition was dominated by Michel Platini and he scored the winning goal in extra time in a 3-2 win against Portugal – but only after Domergue had led the way for France.

In the last-four encounter in Marseille the defender smashed in a free-kick, then equalised after a Rui Jordão double had turned the game around for Portugal.

This was the undoubted highlight of Domergue's relatively short international career.

1992

KARL-HEINZ RIEDLE

Striker Riedle was involved in all the key moments for Germany as they beat hosts Sweden 3-2 in Solna.

It was Riedle who was fouled just outside the box, allowing Thomas Hässler to curl home a wonderful free-kick before Riedle found space in the area to double the lead.

A Sweden penalty reduced the arrears only for Riedle to put the result beyond doubt two minutes from time with a sweet finish, despite a late Kennet Andersson consolation.

HENRIK LARSEN

Goalkeeper Peter Schmeichel grabbed the headlines with a penalty save from Marco van Basten that decided the shoot-out, but it was Larsen whose goals got Denmark that far.

Larsen nodded in the first of the match and smashed home to give Denmark a 2-1 half-time lead after Dennis Bergkamp had equalised for the Netherlands.

Frank Rijkaard's late leveller sent the game to extra time, then penalties, where Larsen was the first man to step forward and convert, though it was Kim Christofte who finished it off from the spot.

1988

OLEH PROTASOV

The Soviet Union kept hopes of a second EURO title alive with a clinical second-half display against Italy and it was Protasov's strike that sealed a place in the final.

A youthful Italian team made life tough, but the deadlock was broken in the 58th minute in Stuttgart when Hennadiy Lytovchenko weaved his way through to score.

Four minutes later, as the rain continued to fall, the Soviet Union broke quickly and when the ball arrived at Protasov's feet on the edge of the box, he swept it home expertly to complete a 2-0 victory.

MARCO VAN BASTEN

Dutch striker Van Basten had many big moments during the 1988 tournament and he saved two for the semi-final.

Taking on the hosts in Hamburg, West Germany and the Netherlands traded penalties in the second half, Ronald Koeman equalising after Van Basten had been tripped.

With time ticking away, Van Basten latched onto a through-ball and stretched to steer the ball past Eike Immel to make it 2-1. He would famously go on to have a great impact in the final too.

1996

PETR KOUBA

The Czech Republic's adventure continued at EURO '96 as goalkeeper Kouba made the decisive save in the penalty shoot-out against France.

Both sides had players missing and a cautious encounter went the distance where each team scored five out of five penalties before Kouba saved with his legs from Reynald Pedros, allowing Miroslav Kadlec to slot the winner.

STEFAN KUNTZ

A goal in the first half and a converted penalty in the shoot-out made Kuntz's contribution a crucial one as they beat hosts England at Wembley.

Alan Shearer had nodded in an early goal, but Kuntz replied swiftly, showing his predatory instincts to be the first to react when a ball was played across the box.

Both sides had chances to win it, but penalties were needed to separate the sides, Kuntz scoring Germany's fifth. That piled the pressure on Gareth Southgate who missed, allowing Andreas Möller to take the winning kick.

From the everyday game to the beautiful game

Your offical partner for fresh fruit and vegetables

2000

ZINEDINE ZIDANE

When a calm head was needed, Zidane provided it as his golden-goal penalty decided France's semi-final against Portugal.

Nuno Gomes had struck a superb opener for the Portuguese before a lovely finish from Thierry Henry squared things up.

Both sides had big chances to win it, but with a penalty shoot-out looming it turned out only one spot-kick was needed in extra time after Abel Xavier handled in the box and Zidane stepped up to make it 2-1 with only three minutes left.

FRANCESCO TOLDO

Italy's goalkeeper had a day to remember as his spectacular display of penalty-saving almost single-handedly ousted the Netherlands.

It didn't look good for Italy when Gianluca Zambrotta was dismissed in the first half, leaving his team-mates to battle through the rest of the match, including extra time, one player short.

To make matters worse, Italy conceded two penalties, the first of which Toldo saved before Patrick Kluivert struck the post with the second.

Toldo saved two more in the shoot-out to send Italy into the final.

2004

MANICHE

Maniche scored one of the most spectacular goals ever seen at a EURO to help Portugal see off the Netherlands on home soil.

Cristiano Ronaldo had headed the Portuguese into the lead, but Maniche provided the most memorable moment of the match as he collected a short corner and fizzed a strike into the far top corner.

A Jorge Andrade own goal narrowed the gap, but Portugal held on to a 2-1 victory.

TRAIANOS DELLAS

It was a game for defenders when Greece and the Czech Republic met in Porto – but it was in the opposition's penalty area where centre-back Dellas ultimately made the difference.

A tense encounter remained scoreless after 90 minutes and with the silver goal rule in force, neither team wanted to make the crucial mistake in extra time.

It was perfect timing in the end from Dellas as he headed in from a corner right at the end of the first period of extra time and there was no time for the Czechs to respond.

THE TASTE YOU DESERVE
WHEN YOU CROSS
EVERYTHING YOU CAN

OFFICIAL PARTNER

2008

PHILIPP LAHM

There were two late stings in the tail of a fabulously entertaining match in Basel, but it was Lahm and Germany who enjoyed it most.

Turkey began the scoring through Uğur Boral only for Bastian Schweinsteiger to flick in an equaliser and Germany took control through a towering header from Miroslav Klose with just over ten minutes to go.

The grandstand finish was about to begin and after Semih Şentürk had squeezed in an equaliser, it was future captain Lahm's moment to shine as he burst forward from the left-back position, traded passes with Thomas Hitzlsperger and then finished expertly to win the game 3-2.

ANDRÉS INIESTA

As a storm surrounded the Ernst-Happel-Stadion in Vienna, Spain kept their composure and provided the moments of class to beat Russia 3-0.

Man of the match Iniesta's fantastic pass set up midfield team-mate Xavi Hernández to open the scoring in the second half and Spain never looked back.

Iniesta and co kept control as Daniel Güiza and David Silva widened the margin of victory.

2012

IKER CASILLAS

Knockout matches often give goalkeepers the chance to be the hero – especially when ties go to penalties – and legendary Spain captain Casillas had a match to remember against Portugal.

The Real Madrid man proved unbeatable during the match itself and when the game went all the way to spot-kicks, he piled the pressure on Portugal by making a magnificent save from the first shot he faced, from João Moutinho.

When Bruno Alves missed Portugal's fourth, Spain were in the final.

MARIO BALOTELLI

Two goals from Balotelli settled a heavyweight contest in which Italy beat Germany 2-1 in Warsaw.

Balotelli was the type of player who could frustrate and delight in equal measure, but there was no doubt that he was the toast of Italy on this day.

Both of his goals came in the first half, the opener an unstoppable header from an Antonio Cassano cross, the second an emphatic finish after running onto a ball over the top.

Mesut Özil's penalty came too late to cause any real concerns.

What unites us matters.

That's why we're your partner.

Football unites us. This is where we share our passion, our values and a willingness to give it our all – no matter where we come from or whatever else we might believe in. That is why we are supporting the European Football Championship and its Volunteer Programme in our role as National Insurance Partner of UEFA EURO 2024™ and Partner of the German National Team. Together we want to turn this tournament in the heart of Europe into a football festival for everyone.

ERGO

Simple because it matters.

2016

CRISTIANO RONALDO

Portugal legend Ronaldo reached several milestones as he scored and assisted to help his team into the final in France.

Wales were the opponents as Ronaldo became the first man to appear in three EURO semi-finals and his incredible leap and powerful header opened the scoring and brought him level with Michel Platini as the top EURO scorer of all time with nine.

Three minutes later he became the provider, sending the ball into the box and Nani diverted it into the net to round off a 2-0 win.

ANTOINE GRIEZMANN

The Marseille crowd saw Griezmann score his fifth and sixth goals of UEFA EURO 2016 to earn a place in the final.

Opponents Germany had plenty of chances of their own, but Griezmann was at his clinical best, serving an early warning as he orchestrated a move that he began on the halfway line and ended with him drawing a fabulous save from Manuel Neuer. He broke the deadlock just before half-time, converting a penalty following a Bastian Schweinsteiger handball, and poked home a second with 18 minutes to go to complete a 2-0 success.

2020

GIANLUIGI DONNARUMMA

Italy goalkeeper Donnarumma had a huge influence over his side's progress at UEFA EURO 2020 and his contribution was crucial again in this semi-final against Spain.

After Federico Chiesa's stunning goal, Álvaro Morata played a brilliant one-two with Dani Olmo to slot past Donnarumma as the game finished 1-1 and went to penalties.

Donnarumma would then get the better of Morata in the penalty shoot-out, making a brilliant save as Italy held their nerve to win 4-2.

RAHEEM STERLING

He may not have scored, but Sterling had a big say in the outcome of England's match against Denmark at Wembley.

Mikkel Damsgaard had scored a stunning free-kick for the Danes by the time Sterling drew the first big save from Kasper Schmeichel. The Danish keeper was powerless to prevent the equaliser though as Sterling's presence in the box forced Simon Kjær into an own goal.

When the game went to extra time, it was Sterling who took the game by the scruff of the neck. He was felled as he tried to find an opening in the area and Harry Kane swept in the rebound from his own saved penalty to complete a 2-1 win.

CHART TOP

PEIRS

CELEBRATING THE MEN WHO ETCHED THEIR NAMES IN HISTORY BY TOP-SCORING AT A EURO

NINE

One man stands head and shoulders above the rest when it comes to dominating a EURO with his goalscoring, **Michel Platini.** The France captain scored in each of his five appearances at the 1984 UEFA European Championship, including the winner against Denmark, successive hat-tricks against Belgium and Yugoslavia, a dramatic extra-time winner in the semi-final, topped off with the opener in the final.

France's semi-final against Portugal in 1984 was settled by a goal from Michel Platini

Antoine Griezmann was in scintillating form in 2016

Marco van Basten's fifth strike at the 1988 finals was also his best

SIX

Playing a EURO on home soil must provide extra inspiration for French forwards because 32 years after Platini scored nine, **Antoine Griezmann** was top-scoring at UEFA EURO 2016 in France. Unfortunately for Griezmann, his goals were not enough to earn a winner's medal, but his six strikes make him the second highest goalscorer at a single EURO. After one goal in the group stage, the Atlético de Madrid man came alive in the knockout rounds, netting twice against the Republic of Ireland, chipping in with another against Iceland, then striking both of France's goals in the semi-final against Germany.

Milan Baroš showed his range of finishing skills in 2004

Savo Milosević hit five in 2000

FIVE

Five is a very healthy amount of goals to score at a major championship, especially when the highest number of games you can play is five and you weren't even selected to start the first game, as was the case for **Marco van Basten** in 1988.

The best way for a forward to push his claims for selection is to score goals, so when he started the Netherlands' second game, against England, a fantastic hat-trick meant he could be overlooked no more. Nobody will need reminding that the pick of his five goals was saved for last as he volleyed gloriously into the net from the tightest of angles against the Soviet Union in the final.

The next man to manage five in a single tournament did so eight years later. **Alan Shearer** scored in four out of five of England's matches at EURO '96, the pick of the bunch being when he blasted his second past Edwin van der Sar to round off a great team move in a 4-1 win over the Netherlands.

Savo Milošević scored twice in FR Yugoslavia's opening match at UEFA EURO 2000 and another one in each of his country's remaining matches, including when they were knocked out in the quarter-finals. The five goals he scored at that tournament were matched by **Patrick Kluivert**, who struck three of the Netherlands' goals in that 6-1 win over Milošević's side. The Dutch striker had also scored against Denmark and France, with the latter of those a particularly sweet strike that helped his country top the group ahead of the world champions.

There were no tap-ins among **Milan Baroš**'s five goals at UEFA EURO 2004 as he stood alone as the top scorer. He netted in each group game and twice in the Czech Republic's quarter-final against Denmark, a mix of fierce piledrivers and delicate finishes worthy of one of Europe's top strikers at the time.

Five was also the magic number at UEFA EURO 2020 as Portugal's **Cristiano Ronaldo** and Czech striker **Patrik Schick** stood above the rest. Ronaldo walked away with the Top Scorer award by virtue of providing an assist too as he rattled in three penalties among his tally. Schick's goals showed the full range of his abilities, scoring with both feet and his head, though the best came in the Czechs' opening match when he sent a shot into the net from just inside the Scotland half in a 2-0 win.

In diesem Sommer wird Hopfen und Malz gegrillt!

Mann, is' das 'ne Wurst!

FOUR

Three players have ended a EURO as top scorer with four goals, and two of those players were called Müller.

First up, in 1972, was one of the greatest goalscorers of all time, **Gerd Müller**. In the days when the finals only consisted of two matches, in this case a semi-final and a final, 'Der Bomber' scored twice in a 2-1 win against Belgium, then struck two more against the Soviet Union to help one of the best ever West Germany teams to the title.

Dieter Müller wasn't quite able to help his country to back-to-back honours, but nobody could doubt the contribution he gave to the cause. He put on one of the greatest performances by a substitute in EURO history as he came off the bench in the 79th minute to score a hat-trick against Yugoslavia, then scored again in the final, only for Czechoslovakia to win the penalty shoot-out.

Fast forward 32 years to UEFA EURO 2008 and Spain forward **David Villa** was in the form of his life, spearheading one of the greatest international sides in history as they marched relentlessly towards the title. A hat-trick in his side's opening match against Russia accounted for most of his goals, which he supplemented with a dramatic late winner against Sweden, but an injury in the semi-final prevented him from lining up in the decider against Germany.

David Villa was in the form of his life in 2008

Fernando Torres' three goals in 2012 included one in the final as Spain beat Italy

THREE

It was David Villa's strike partner, **Fernando Torres**, who then took centre stage in that 2008 final, scoring the winning goal, and that momentum carried him into the 2012 edition where he claimed three more goals to finish joint-top of the scoring chart. He was handed the Top Scorer trophy after claiming an assist and getting his goals despite being on the pitch for the shortest amount of time, one of those goals coming in the final again.

Five other players finished level on three goals, including the evergreen **Cristiano Ronaldo**. The Portuguese legend scored at vital times, grabbing both goals in a 2-1 win over the Netherlands to ensure progress to the knockout rounds before securing the only goal in the quarter-final against the Czech Republic.

Italy made it to the final that year and **Mario Balotelli**'s goals were crucial, particularly the two he scored in the 2-1 semi-final win over Germany, to add to the volley he fired into the Republic of Ireland net during the group phase.

Another Mario, in this case **Mario Gómez**, turned out to be Germany's goalscorer-in-chief in 2012. The only goal in the game against Portugal, and both of the Germans' goals in a 2-1 win over the Netherlands, helped his country to top a tough group.

Mario Mandžukić made it a trio of high-performing Marios in 2012, though his two goals against the Republic of Ireland and one against Italy failed to help Croatia beyond the group stage.

Last but not least, two strikes from **Alan Dzagoev** helped Russia to beat the Czech Republic 4-1 with a further goal earning a point against Poland, but it wasn't quite enough to secure a place in the quarter-finals.

The first time a player topped the charts with three goals at a EURO was in 1980. That year West Germany's **Klaus Allofs** did all the hard work in one game, scoring a hat-trick in a very entertaining match against the Netherlands which finished 3-2.

In 1992 there were four players tied with three goals as joint-top scorers.

Home favourite **Tomas Brolin** was among them as he delighted Swedish fans with winning goals over Denmark and England in the group stage before scoring once in the 3-2 semi-final defeat by Germany.

His stand-out moment was that goal against England, playing two one-twos before finding the top corner with a shot from the outside of his boot to clinch a 2-1 win.

Karl-Heinz Riedle was the star of the aforementioned semi-final between Sweden and Germany, with two goals and a key contribution to the other – these goals coming after he'd scored the opener in a 2-0 win over Scotland in the group stage.

Dennis Bergkamp also found the net against Scotland – the only goal of the game – before scoring the third in the Netherlands' 3-1 win over Germany.

He added another in the semi-final against Denmark and side-footed in his penalty in a losing cause during the shoot-out.

The fourth man to hit three goals at EURO 1992 would have ended up the happiest as he helped Denmark to the title. **Henrik Larsen**'s most memorable input came when his two goals took the semi-final against the Netherlands to penalties, though his first goal in the tournament came in a group-stage win over France.

Betano

SPORTWETTEN

OFFICIAL SPONSOR

TWO

Opportunities to rack up significant numbers of goals were fewer in the early days of the European Championship finals, with there only being semi-finals, a final and a third-place play-off. That understandably meant that top scorers in those early tournaments generally became so without scoring goals galore.

In the first three EUROs it only took two goals to lead the way, though the honour of being the sharpest shooter was usually shared.

Five players scored twice during the first tournament in 1960 and the free-scoring semi-final between France and Yugoslavia, which finished 5-4 to the latter, saw **François Heutte** and **Dražan Jerković** get two each. **Milan Galić** opened the scoring that day, as he did during the final to take his tally to two.

The other semi-final was a personal triumph for **Valentin Ivanov**, who scored two of the Soviet Union's goals against Czechoslovakia. **Viktor Ponedelnik** added the third in that 3-0 win before claiming the winner in the final.

There were fewer goals scored in 1964, but three players got two each. Two of those men were Hungarians, **Deszö Novák** leaving it late before scoring twice in extra time against Denmark in the third-place play-off. **Ferenc Bene** got the other Hungary goal in that 3-1 win, having opened his account in the semi-final defeat by Spain.

Jesús María Pereda scored the opening goal for the Spaniards in that game and did likewise in the final against the Soviet Union.

There were only seven goals scored at the 1968 finals despite the fact that there were five matches because the final went to a replay.

The only man to score more than once was Yugoslavia's **Dragan Džajić**. His fantastic goal decided the 1-0 semi-final win over England and three days later he scored in the final that finished 1-1 against Italy.

Sadly, he couldn't get on the scoresheet in the replay but he demonstrated his longevity by scoring a further two goals when Yugoslavia next made it to a EURO finals in 1976.

Valentin Ivanov was one of five players to score twice in 1960

TOP SCORERS – TOURNAMENT BY TOURNAMENT

1960: — **2 GOALS**
Milan Galić (Yugoslavia)
François Heutte (France)
Valentin Ivanov (Soviet Union)
Dražan Jerković (Yugoslavia)
Viktor Ponedelnik (Soviet Union)

1964: — **2 GOALS**
Ferenc Bene (Hungary)
Deszö Novák (Hungary)
Jesús María Pereda (Spain)

1968: — **2 GOALS**
Dragan Džajić (Yugoslavia)

1972: — **4 GOALS**
Gerd Müller (West Germany)

1976: — **4 GOALS**
Dieter Müller (West Germany)

1980: — **3 GOALS**
Klaus Allofs (West Germany)

1984: — **9 GOALS**
Michel Platini (France)

1988: — **5 GOALS**
Marco van Basten (Netherlands)

1992: — **3 GOALS**
Dennis Bergkamp (Netherlands)
Tomas Brolin (Sweden)
Henrik Larsen (Denmark)
Karl-Heinz Riedle (Germany)

1996: — **5 GOALS**
Alan Shearer (England)

2000: — **5 GOALS**
Patrick Kluivert (Netherlands)
Savo Milošević (Yugoslavia)

2004: — **5 GOALS**
Milan Baroš (Czech Republic)

2008: — **4 GOALS**
David Villa (Spain)

2012: — **3 GOALS**
Fernando Torres (Spain)
Alan Dzagoev (Russia)
Mario Gomez (Germany)
Mario Mandžukić (Croatia)
Mario Balotelli (Italy)
Cristiano Ronaldo (Portugal)

2016: — **6 GOALS**
Antoine Griezmann (France)

2020: — **5 GOALS**
Cristiano Ronaldo (Portugal)
Patrik Schick (Czechia)

GERMANY'S PARTY

There's nothing like football for stirring emotions and creating memories that will last a lifetime.

A month of fantastic action on the pitch is setting the platform for fans from all over the continent to descend on Germany and have the time of their lives.

Whether in the stadium, at fan parks or around the host cities, supporters have mingled with locals and added colour and energy to a tournament that has entertained right from the start.

Here is just a small sample of images that prove that the game just wouldn't be the same without fans...

ENDLICH ANSTOSSEN

Bitte

Bitte ein Bit

UEFA
EURO2024
GERMANY

Bitburger

Offizielles Bier der UEFA EURO 2024™

HOW UEFA REINVESTS EURO REVENUE INTO FOOTBALL DEVELOPMENT

This year marks the 20th anniversary of HatTrick, UEFA's flagship development programme.

Since its launch in 2004, UEFA HatTrick has evolved into one of global sport's largest solidarity schemes, channelling €2.6bn into football development programmes. By reinvesting men's EURO revenue back into the game through projects at national association level, it has become an important driver of UEFA's not-for-profit mission.

This year is a milestone one for HatTrick, not only because it marks its 20th anniversary, but also the start of a new cycle, its sixth. This one is set to redistribute more revenue than ever, with EURO 2024 projected to generate €935m – a 21% increase on the previous edition – for investment in football development projects across Europe over the next four years.

Before every HatTrick cycle is approved, UEFA engages in months of consultation with its 55 national associations to better understand the current footballing landscape and their changing needs. The last cycle is evaluated but also the previous cycles to spot longer term trends.

LEADING FACILITIES

One of the most significant ways in which HatTrick has transformed the European football landscape is through investment in infrastructure. By helping associations build new facilities and modernise existing ones, HatTrick has helped to level the playing field and strengthen the footballing pyramid across the continent.

At the very top level, HatTrick funding has contributed to

the construction or development of 35 national stadiums, meaning more than 60% of national football grounds in Europe have been built or modernised thanks to the programme. This includes improvements in player and spectator safety, as well as improving accessibility for people with disabilities.

CASE STUDY: GEORGIA

To complement these stadiums, HatTrick investment has also helped construct 34 national training centres. The most recent of these can be found at first-time EURO final tournament qualifiers Georgia, where HatTrick funding contributed to the construction of five national training centres in the build-up to the European Under-21 Championship finals, co-hosted with Romania in the summer of 2023.

"The legacy of the tournament is invaluable for Georgian football," says Levan Kobiashvili, president of the Georgian Football Federation. "The newly built and renovated high-quality training and playing facilities are already serving

"The legacy of the tournament is invaluable for Georgian football"

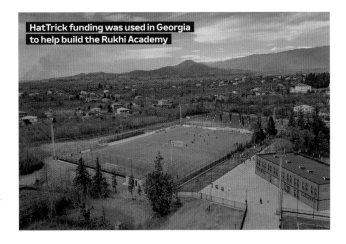

HatTrick funding was used in Georgia to help build the Rukhi Academy

to develop the domestic game." The results have already started to pay off as witnessed by the country's superb EURO finals debut this summer.

Looking further down the pyramid, HatTrick has funded thousands of playing pitches across the continent, ensuring everyone is given the chance to play football, regardless of where they live. More than 1,000 full-size and 3,000 mini pitches have been constructed with HatTrick funding since 2004, an average of more than 70 pitches per member association.

ACCELERATING DEVELOPMENT

Infrastructure is obviously an important aspect of HatTrick's impact, but the scheme also recognises the need to invest in the action on the pitch, not just the pitch itself. Over its 20 years of existence, HatTrick has funded more than 700 women's football development programmes, with nearly 60% of those projects creating new opportunities for women and girls to get into football. UEFA's investment in women's football has jumped by 50% since 2019, and HatTrick has played an important part in that increase.

More than 400 elite youth football projects have also been funded by HatTrick, helping associations develop talent pathways and raise the standards of youth coaching, while giving players the opportunity to compete at a higher level earlier in their careers. The Football in Schools programme, meanwhile, has reached 2.4 million children in more than 44,000 schools, with 100,000 teachers given training to deliver football sessions.

BROADER IMPACT

Away from the pitch, HatTrick has funded more than 500 social and environmental projects, helping to leverage football's influence as a wider force for good. As part of these efforts to tackle football's climate impact, recent HatTrick-funded schemes have addressed waste reduction, renewable energy transition, sustainable construction, and public transport uptake, among many others. Socially, HatTrick has funded projects aimed at eliminating discrimination, improving mental health, supporting refugees, safeguarding children, and many more.

When HatTrick was launched in 2004, few would have foreseen the depth and breadth of its impact on the European football landscape over the next 20 years. The sixth cycle of HatTrick will undoubtedly be bigger and better than ever, and with it, so will football.

STRAUSS.COM
NOW SHIPPING GLOBALLY

OFFICIAL UEFA EURO 2024™ WORKWEAR PARTNER

HIGH-VIS – TEAMWEAR
AMBITION

STRAUSS WORKS WORLDWIDE

WHAT'S IT LIKE TO REFEREE AT A EUROPEAN CHAMPIONSHIP?

WE SPEAK WITH BJÖRN KUIPERS, THE MAN IN THE MIDDLE FOR THE UEFA EURO 2020 FINAL, WHO IS HELPING TO GUIDE THIS YEAR'S OFFICIALS THROUGH THE TOURNAMENT

There are few better ways to retire from the game than by being involved in a European Championship final.

That was the honour bestowed upon Björn Kuipers at EURO 2020, when the Dutchman was selected to referee the decider between England and eventual winners Italy at London's Wembley Stadium.

"It was a fantastic moment, one to never forget," Kuipers recalls. "I had refereed other finals but EURO was not on the list, so it was really something special and we got very positive feedback as a team of officials. I had already decided it would be my last game, I didn't want to be past my sell-by date, and it was the perfect moment to finish."

Kuipers is now a member of UEFA's referee committee, and is part of the support team that appoints officials for EURO 2024, helping to guide them through an intense period that begins well before the tournament kicks off.

"If you are selected for the EURO, then you are one of the best referees in Europe, and therefore the world," Kuipers says. "It is a special honour, but it also means that you have to

perform. When the referees come to Germany, the focus is completely on football and they will be prepared in the best possible way."

The matches come thick and fast, and just like players, referees eagerly await their match appointments. When selected, they are officiating at the most technically advanced EURO yet, with connected ball technology added to VAR, semi-automated offside and goal-line technology for the first time.

VAR is used carefully, with minimum interference to avoid only clear errors, while referees are instructed to be firm on dissent and unsporting behaviour.

"We will instruct our referees to be strict with the players," Kuipers says. "The most important thing is respect and fair play. The players and coaches are examples for young people, so they cannot react to decisions in an unacceptable way."

This message was communicated to coaches at a pre-tournament meeting, and Kuipers and his refereeing colleagues also visited squads ahead of the kick-off to discuss key issues.

UEFA's Be a Referee! campaign is inspiring young people across Europe to pick up the whistle and sample life as a match official.

We are looking to recruit 40,000 new referees each season to help support the running of the game at grassroots level. As well as a good understanding of the game, officials need a strong sense of fairness, impartiality and the ability to make quick decisions under pressure.

"To become a referee, you need to love football," says Björn Kuipers. "We want strong characters with good body language and a positive attitude."

Scan the QR code to find out more!

THE MAGNIFICENCE OF MUNICH

Germany's third largest city is the perfect example of somewhere that embraces its past and looks to the future all at the same time.

Grand baroque buildings and age-old festivals sit alongside futuristic cars and modern tourist attractions in a city where everyone can feel comfortable.

Its location in the south of Germany, around 50 kilometres from the Austrian border with the Alps in the distance and picturesque lakes nearby, means there's lots to explore – but there's so much to see and do in the centre of Munich too.

The name Munich means 'home of the monks' and stems from the Benedictine monastery that was found there in the mid-8th century.

The region has a history that goes back even further, but it wasn't until 1158 that the place was first mentioned in a document and the market town grew to be capital of Bavaria by 1506.

Like many places, centuries of history include ravages of wars, disease and other difficulties, but it always bounced back and in the 19th century it was a centre of arts, literature and music with elegant Neoclassical buildings.

It was in 1810 that the first Oktoberfest took place in honour of the marriage of King Ludwig I of Bavaria to Princess Therese of Saxe-Hildburghausen.

It is a festival that is still annually celebrated and brings tourism and wealth to a city that had to be largely rebuilt in the aftermath of World War II, though much of its original street grid remains and some of the more historic buildings were restored.

SCHLOSS NYMPHENBURG

This sport-mad city hosted the Olympic Games in 1972 and retains the Olympic Stadium, while the hugely-impressive Munich Football Arena and the Grunwalder Stadion illustrate just how keen Munich is on its football.

Places to visit on a trip to Munich are too many to list, but Marienplatz at the heart of the old town is a great place to start. There you can find St Peterskirche where people fit enough can climb 306 steps up the steeple for fabulous views.

The Kunstareal district is an area of rich culture with one museum or gallery after another, including the Alte Pinakothek, which houses a huge collection of paintings, and the Pinakothek der Moderne, where you'll find originals from the likes of Andy Warhol and Pablo Picasso.

Whether your interest is the motor-led surroundings of BMW Welt or the palatial setting of Schloss Nymphenburg, time spent in Munich is time well spent.

FASCINATING FACT

◆

When he was just one year old, Albert Einstein – one of the most influential scientists of all time – and his family moved to Munich, where he spent his childhood.

FIVE THINGS TO EXPERIENCE IN MUNICH

⌃ MARIENPLATZ

The central square of Munich, all roads seem to lead to Marienplatz, which is why it is always a hive of activity. Big events including football celebrations and Christmas markets happen here and many of the city's central attractions are only a short walk away.

⌄ VIKTUALIENMARKT

In the heart of the old town, this was originally a farmers' market, but the range of goods on sale here is now far more extensive. There are a series of fountains featuring statues of local heroes and a maypole which incorporates images that reflect life in Munich, such as a horse and cart transporting beer, Oktoberfest scenes and the flag of the city.

⌄ ENGLISH GARDEN

Covering an area of around 640 football pitches, the park connects the greenland of the north of Munich with the old town and includes the Kleinhesseloher lake, Japanese Tea House and the chance to surf along the waves of the Eisbach river.

⌃ OLYMPIC PARK

The perfect legacy from the 1972 Games, the Olympic Park is true to its sporting roots with facilities for all manner of sports. The centrepiece is the Olympic Stadium, but the 291-metre-high Olympic Tower is the city's greatest vantage point and includes a revolving restaurant.

⌃ HOFBRÄUHAUS

Open every day of the year, possibly the most famous beer house in Germany has to be visited at least once. There's a fantastic beer garden, a main hall complete with oompah band, giant kitchen and also quieter corners – with a gift shop to visit once your beer tokens have run out!

BE DAZZLED BY DORTMUND

A vibrant and modern city on first inspection, Dortmund has a history that goes back well over 1,000 years and has a story to tell.

Those centuries have seen the fortunes of the city's inhabitants rise and fall, and the predominant industries have changed over time – but the character of this place can't be questioned.

Sited in North Rhine-Westphalia in western Germany, original mentions of what would develop into a trade hub call the place Throtmanni in 885 and it was classified as a city in 1220.

Its position on the Ruhr river meant it became a prosperous area in the 14th century, but the Thirty Years' War saw a reversal in its fortunes until the development of its coal and iron ore industries in the 19th century which, along with the completion of the canal network, stimulated huge growth.

Moving closer to modern times, following the decline of those traditional industries, the region has concentrated on technology, finance, education and service industries to make it one of the most dynamic cities in the country. For all that dynamism, one of the greatest strings to its bow is the fact that Dortmund is such a green city with nearly half of the area made up of parks, woodland, waterways and other green spaces.

The city centre skyline has lots of distinctive features including the Dortmunder U, where a giant letter draws attention to what was once the centre of the city's brewing industry. There is also the Florian Tower, a giant telecommunications building of around 220 metres in height which was once the highest freestanding structure in the country.

There is also plenty to excite historians with

four medieval churches – the Propsteikirche, the Reinoldikirche, the Marienkirche and the Petrikirche – and four castles, plus the ruins of ancient fortresses.

The 'Dortmund Treasure', a collection of around 400 gold coins, can be found in the Museum of Art and Cultural History, one of several museums the city has to offer.

At its heart, Dortmund is about the people, and visitors can feel more like a permanent resident when tucking into the local delicacies of Pfefferpotthast, a time-honoured Westphalian beef stew; Salzkuchen with Mett, which is a salty baked roll filled with seasoned minced pork and onions; or Pommes Schranke, fries topped with mayonnaise and ketchup in a way that visually resembles a railroad barrier (Schranke).

And we've not even mentioned beer...

FASCINATING FACT

◆

Dortmund is home to the largest canal port in Europe. Opened in 1899, it now consists of 10 docks and has a pier length of 11 km, and connects local industry to the North Sea.

FIVE THINGS TO EXPERIENCE IN DORTMUND

⌃ REINOLDIKIRCHE

One of several ancient churches, Reinoldikirche dates back to 1280, is claimed to be the oldest and was named after the patron saint of Dortmund. There is a statue of Reinold within the building, a beautiful altar and a bell tower which offers great views.

⌄ GERMAN FOOTBALL MUSEUM

The fact that Germany's national football museum is in Dortmund shows how closely linked the city and the global game are. Situated next to the main train station, the history of the Bundesliga and the national team are main themes – and an interactive experience awaits. The place is perfectly summed up by its motto: One ball, 1,000 stories.

⌄ DORTMUNDER U

What was once the symbol of the dominant brewing industry in the city, the gleaming giant U still draws attention to what is now a home for art and creativity. Artwork from the last two centuries is one of the main draws, but there's also a rooftop terrace with spectacular views.

⌃ BRAUEREI-MUSEUM DORTMUND

This museum is a tribute to the influence of the brewing industry in Dortmund, with a particular focus on the golden years from 1950-70, but also going much further back. A 1920s bar, a beer truck from 1922 and bottling machines from the 1950s are among the original historical items on display.

⌃ PHOENIX LAKE

An example of how to give a once-industrial part of town a new lease of life, Phoenix Lake was built on the site of an old steel works and is now a leisure hub for locals and visitors. Its promenades offer space for exercise, relaxation and indulgence at one of the many restaurants and cafés – while water sports are also available on the lake itself.

Nationaler Partner

Günstig reisen mit den Sparpreisen.

bahn.de/sparpreise

Ab 12⁹⁹€*

*Solange der Vorrat reicht. Im DB Fernverkehr (ICE, IC/EC). Buchbar bis 30.09.

UEFA's environmental, social and governance strategy covers various sustainable development goals

CLIMATE FUND LEAVES A EURO 2024 LEGACY

In the lead-up to this summer's tournament, UEFA launched a climate fund which gave German amateur football clubs and regional associations the opportunity to apply for environmental projects support.

The fund, which was announced under the slogan 'United by Football – Together for Nature', had a total of €7m earmarked for distribution. Clubs were able to suggest projects relating to one or more of the following four categories: energy, water, waste management and mobility.

As Michele Uva, UEFA social & environmental sustainability director, explains: "UEFA's climate fund offer has inspired thousands of grassroots clubs all over Germany, confirming the appeal of the programme and showing the acceleration potential of this initiative. The investment of €7m will contribute to a sustainable legacy for the EURO 2024 tournament, making a significant impact on reducing CO_2 emissions and supporting climate protection. It's great to see our environmental, social and governance strategy further coming to life, catalysing actions in support of the environment."

The fund was an instant hit following its launch on 8 January with thousands of clubs in Germany submitting applications. Popular projects included the installation of LED floodlights, photovoltaic solar panels, smart irrigation system, sharing stations for e-cars and heat pumps.

Major efforts have been made to reduce the environmental impact of the tournament through the targeted measures and investments laid out in the UEFA EURO 2024 ESG strategy.

€7M IS HELPING GERMAN AMATEUR FOOTBALL CLUBS TO DEVELOP ACTION PROJECTS

The €7m total is based on €25 being donated for each tonne of CO_2 emissions predicted to be produced in connection with UEFA EURO 2024. This significant investment in projects that will mitigate CO_2 emissions over the long term will strengthen UEFA EURO 2024's legacy both within the German football community and for the environment.

Funding applications were able to be requested for any sum up to a maximum of €250,000 with clubs only having to finance a maximum of €5,000 or 10% of the total project costs themselves. A simplified application procedure applied to requests for less than €25,000, and applicants were allowed to combine various smaller projects in a single application.

More information: **www.uefa.com/sustainability/ euro2024climatefund**

"It's the first time that a climate fund has been set up for a EURO tournament. It's a great investment for the sake of our climate and in our football infrastructure in Germany. On behalf of the entire German football family, we would like to thank UEFA for the initiative and its implementation"

Heike Ullrich, German Football Association (DFB) general secretary

SENIOR STARS

ALBANIA
◆

Oldest player: Ansi Agolli, 33 years 252 days (vs Romania, EURO 2016)
Oldest scorer: Armando Sadiku, 25 years 23 days (vs Romania, EURO 2016)

AUSTRIA
◆

Oldest player: Ivica Vastic, 38 years 257 days (vs Poland, EURO 2008)
Oldest scorer: Ivica Vastic, 38 years 257 days (vs Poland, EURO 2008)

BELGIUM
◆

Oldest player: Lorenzo Staelens, 36 years 50 days (vs Turkey, EURO 2000)
Oldest scorer: Julien Cools, 33 years 123 days (vs Spain, EURO '80)

CROATIA
◆

Oldest player: Niko Kovač, 36 years 249 days (vs Turkey, EURO 2008)
Oldest scorer: Luka Modrić, 35 years 286 days (vs Scotland, EURO 2020)

CZECHIA
◆

Oldest player: Tomáš Rosický, 35 years 257 days (vs Croatia, EURO 2016)
Oldest scorer: Jan Koller, 35 years 77 days (vs Turkey, EURO 2008)

DENMARK
◆

Oldest player: Morten Olsen, 38 years 308 days (vs Italy, EURO '88)
Oldest scorer: Martin Braithwaite, 30 years 21 days (vs Wales, EURO 2020)

ENGLAND
◆

Oldest player: Peter Shilton, 38 years 271 days (vs Netherlands, EURO '88)
Oldest scorer: Trevor Brooking, 31 years 260 days (vs Spain, EURO '80)

FRANCE
◆

Oldest player: Lilian Thuram, 36 years 164 days (vs Netherlands, EURO 2008)
Oldest scorer: Laurent Blanc, 34 years 205 days (vs Denmark, EURO 2000)

Before a ball was kicked at UEFA EURO 2024, the oldest outfield player to have appeared at a European Championship was Germany legend Lothar Matthäus.

The midfield dynamo was 39 years and 91 days old when he played against Portugal at EURO 2000, though that is still nearly a year younger than Hungary goalkeeper Gábor Király, who had long turned 40 when he played against Belgium 16 years later.

The oldest man to find the net was Austria's Ivica Vastic, who was 38 years and 257 days old when he scored from the penalty spot against Poland in 2008.

Using statistics collated by UEFA.com for the 23 competing nations who have appeared at previous EUROs, here are the players who have shown that age is no barrier when it comes to performing at the highest level.

GERMANY

Oldest player: Lothar Matthäus, 39 years 91 days (vs Portugal, EURO 2000)
Oldest scorer: Miroslav Klose, 34 years 13 days (vs Greece, EURO 2012)

HUNGARY

Oldest player: Gábor Király, 40 years 86 days (vs Belgium, EURO 2016)
Oldest scorer: Zoltán Gera, 37 years 61 days (vs Portugal, EURO 2016)

ITALY

Oldest player: Gianluigi Buffon, 38 years 156 days (vs Germany, EURO 2016)
Oldest scorer: Christian Panucci, 35 years 62 days (vs Romania, EURO 2008)

NETHERLANDS

Oldest player: Maarten Stekelenburg, aged 38 years 278 days (vs Czechia, EURO 2020)
Oldest scorer: Giovanni van Bronckhorst, 33 years 125 days (vs Italy, EURO 2008)

POLAND

Oldest player: Jacek Bąk, 35 years 80 days (vs Austria, EURO 2008)
Oldest scorer: Robert Lewandowski, 32 years 306 days (vs Sweden, EURO 2020)

PORTUGAL

Oldest player: Pepe, 38 years 121 days (vs Belgium, EURO 2020)
Oldest scorer: Cristiano Ronaldo, 36 years 138 days (vs France, EURO 2020)

ROMANIA

Oldest player: Lucian Sanmartean, 36 years 98 days (vs Albania, EURO 2016)
Oldest scorer: Dorinel Munteanu, 31 years 361 days (vs England, EURO 2000)

SCOTLAND

Oldest player: David Marshall, 36 years 109 days (vs Croatia, EURO 2020)
Oldest scorer: Ally McCoist, aged 33 years 268 days (vs Switzerland, EURO '96)

SERBIA

Oldest player: Dragan Stojković, 35 years 114 days (vs Netherlands, EURO 2000)
Oldest scorer: Ljubinko Drulović, 31 years 276 days (vs Slovenia, EURO 2000)

SLOVAKIA

Oldest player: Peter Pekarík, aged 34 years 236 days (vs Spain, EURO 2020)
Oldest scorer (for Czechoslovakia): Ladislav Pavlovič, 34 years 92 days (vs France, EURO '60)
Oldest scorer (for Slovakia): Marek Hamšík, 28 years and 324 days (vs Russia, EURO 2016)

SLOVENIA

Oldest player: Darko Milanič, 32 years 183 days (vs Spain, EURO 2000)
Oldest scorer: Zlatko Zahovič, 29 years 138 days (vs Spain, EURO 2000)

SPAIN

Oldest player: Aritz Aduriz, 35 years 137 days (vs Italy, EURO 2016)
Oldest scorer: César Azpilicueta, 31 years 304 days (vs Croatia, EURO 2020)

SWITZERLAND

Oldest player: Pascal Zuberbühler, 37 years 159 days (vs Portugal, EURO 2008)
Oldest scorer: Mario Gavranović, 31 years 216 days (vs France, EURO 2020)

TÜRKIYE

Oldest player: Burak Yılmaz, 35 years 340 days (vs Switzerland, EURO 2020)
Oldest scorer: Burak Yılmaz, 30 years 342 days (vs Czech Republic, EURO 2016)

UKRAINE

Oldest player: Anatoliy Tymoshchuk, 37 years 83 days (vs Poland, EURO 2016)
Oldest scorer: Andriy Shevchenko, 35 years 256 days (vs Sweden, EURO 2012)

EURO
SHOOT-OUTS

NERVOUS TENSION AND EXCITEMENT ARE GUARANTEED – BUT WHICH TEAMS AND INDIVIDUALS HAVE PROVED THEMSELVES TO BE SPOT KINGS SINCE 1976?

Love them or hate them, there's no denying that penalty shoot-outs are full of drama and often play a large part in shaping the destiny of a UEFA European Championship.

In a tournament where there are frequent match-ups between evenly-matched sides where there is so much at stake, there is always a chance it will be difficult to separate teams over 90 or 120 minutes.

In 1976, penalty shoot-outs were introduced to EURO finals for the first time and in every tournament since – except 1988 – spot-kicks have been needed to decide contests.

Indeed, since 1976, seven teams that have gone on to lift the Henri Delaunay Cup have

needed to win a penalty shoot-out en route to glory. Twice the final itself has gone all the way to penalties with Antonín Panenka famously deciding the 1976 outcome in favour of Czechoslovakia with a chip down the middle, while Italy came into this tournament as champions on the back of a shoot-out victory over England at Wembley in the final of UEFA EURO 2020.

Perhaps because of their enduring competitiveness on the EURO stage or because they are regularly involved in tight matches, it is Italy who arrived at this tournament with the most shoot-out experience behind them.

Italy have had the outcome of seven EURO

matches decided on penalties, winning four of them, but they are less successful the longer a contest goes on. They were involved in the two longest shoot-outs in EURO history (18 kicks in each one) losing a third-place play-off to Czechoslovakia 9-8 in 1980 and a quarter-final to Germany 6-5 in 2016.

Given their regular involvement, it comes as little surprise that an Italian – Gianluigi Buffon – has been involved in the joint-highest number of EURO shoot-outs of any goalkeeper, taking part in three, along with the Netherlands' Edwin van der Sar and Switzerland's Yann Sommer.

Only two goalkeepers have finished on the winning side in a shoot-out twice, one of those being Italy's Gianluigi Donnarumma, whose impact resulted in him being named Player of the Tournament at UEFA EURO 2020, and

Spain's Iker Casillas, who was the hero in both 2008 and 2012.

The most saves recorded by individual goalkeepers is three, a benchmark set by Buffon, Casillas, Donnarumma and Spain's Unai Simón.

While history is littered with stories of goalkeepers who have made crucial penalty saves, for those who have had to endure the nervous walk up to the spot at a EURO, the highest number of successful shoot-out kicks by an individual is two, a mark shared by many players, though only two outfielders – Switzerland's Fabian Schär and Italy's Leonardo Bonucci – have stepped up in three different matches.

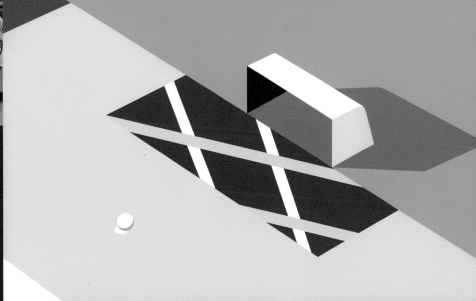

2008 QUARTER-FINAL:
Croatia 1-1 Turkey,
Turkey won 3-1 on pens

2008 QUARTER-FINAL:
Spain 0-0 Italy,
Spain won 4-2 on pens

2012 QUARTER-FINAL:
England 0-0 Italy,
Italy won 4-2 on pens

2012 SEMI-FINAL:
Portugal 0-0 Spain,
Spain won 4-2 on pens

2016 ROUND OF 16:
Poland 1-1 Switzerland,
Poland won 5-4 on pens

2016 QUARTER-FINAL:
Poland 1-1 Portugal,
Portugal won 5-3 on pens

2016 QUARTER-FINAL:
Germany 1-1 Italy,
Germany won 6-5 on pens

2020 ROUND OF 16:
France 3-3 Switzerland,
Switzerland won 5-4 on pens

2020 QUARTER-FINAL:
Switzerland 1-1 Spain,
Spain won 3-1 on pens

2020 SEMI-FINAL:
Italy 1-1 Spain,
Italy won 4-2 on pens

2020 FINAL:
Italy 1-1 England,
Italy won 3-2 on pens

MOST SHOOT-OUTS BY TEAM

7 ITALY

6 SPAIN

5 ENGLAND

4 NETHERLANDS

3 CZECHOSLOVAKIA/CZECH REPUBLIC, FRANCE, WEST GERMANY/GERMANY, PORTUGAL, SWITZERLAND

2 DENMARK, POLAND

1 CROATIA, SWEDEN, TURKEY

While winning via penalties is joyous, losing is devastating, and no country has endured that experience more than England, who have gone out of a EURO four times via that method.

The one country no-one wants to face in a shoot-out is Czechia. Whether part of Czechoslovakia or as an independent nation, they have won all three shoot-outs they have been involved in. The only other country with a 100% record is Turkey, though the 3-1 win against Croatia in 2008 is the only shoot-out they've taken part in.

With the stakes as high as ever, there's every chance the business end of UEFA EURO 2024 will be decided by who deals best with the drama of a penalty shoot-out.

MOST SHOOT-OUT WINS BY TEAM

4 ITALY, SPAIN

3 CZECHOSLOVAKIA/CZECH REPUBLIC

2 WEST GERMANY/GERMANY, PORTUGAL

1 DENMARK, ENGLAND, FRANCE, NETHERLANDS, POLAND, SWITZERLAND, TURKEY

UEFA EURO 2024™ Official Partner

BYD SEAL U DM-i
Super DM Technology

Up to 1080 km	**18.3 kwh**	**5.9 s**
Combined range	Battery capacity	AWD 0–100 km/h

byd.com

BUILD YOUR DREAMS

GET TRAINED SAVE LIVES

Just like Albärt, you can learn how to save a life. Scan the QR code and join a fun online course now!

UEFA

EUROPEAN
RESUSCITATION
COUNCIL

OFFICIAL PARTNER

FIND YOUR DEAL, SCORE YOUR GOAL

What is AliExpress?

As the first exclusive e-commerce platform partner for a UEFA Men's European Football Championship, AliExpress will connect online consumers with this summer's festival of football offering amazing deals and interactive game prizes.

Download the App

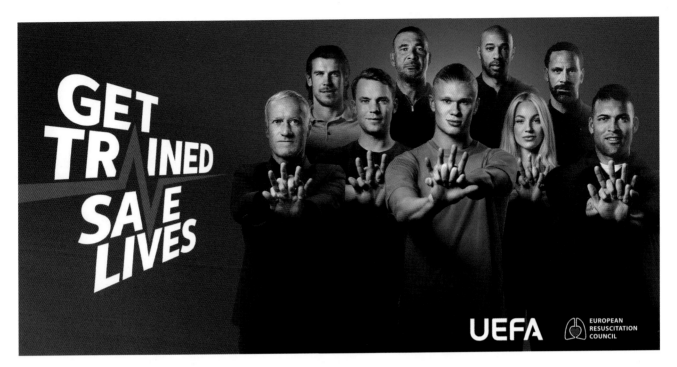

'GET TRAINED, SAVE LIVES': GIVING FOOTBALL FANS CPR SKILLS

UEFA and the European Resuscitation Council (ERC) have teamed up to educate more than 100,000 fans in basic CPR skills and provide in-person training to teams, officials, volunteers and staff at UEFA EURO 2024.

The campaign, 'Get trained, save lives', is being backed by Erling Haaland, Lautaro Martínez, Ana Marković, Ruud Gullit, Gareth Bale, Thierry Henry, Didier Deschamps, Manuel Neuer and Rio Ferdinand. A dedicated platform teaching football fans the basic skills of cardio-pulmonary resuscitation (CPR) in under four minutes has been set up at get-trained.com.

The CPR training on this interactive training module is set in a virtual dressing room and sees Gullit invite football fans to join Haaland, Martínez, Bale, Henry, Ferdinand and Marković on the course. As it commences, interactive questions guide users through the teaching material, with players reacting to and commenting on their answers.

'Get trained, save lives' is part of UEFA's commitment to ensuring the highest standards of medical care and preparedness within football. Since last year, UEFA's minimum medical requirements stipulate that no UEFA match can start without an advanced life support ambulance and three automated external defibrillators (AED) on-site.

Sudden cardiac arrest is the third leading cause of death in Europe, happening to one in 1,000 people every year. In this situation, every minute that passes decreases the chances of survival by 10%. That is why CPR training is so important. Someone nearby when a person suffers a sudden cardiac arrest needs to be able to act quickly to save a life. Getting medical assistance and CPR immediately is crucial because every second counts.

UEFA and the ERC have so far provided hands-on training to 3,000 players, coaches, referees, officials and staff at finals and tournaments. In the build-up to EURO 2024, all participating teams learned how to provide first aid in case of a sudden cardiac arrest.

The campaign has received extra attention during EURO 2024, with a TV commercial and activities in all fan zones across the ten host cities.

"The focus of our campaign launched jointly by UEFA and the ERC is on the power of bystanders — everyday heroes who can turn critical moments into stories of hope and survival. Even a simple chest compression within the first few minutes following a cardiac arrest can significantly increase survival chances and reduce the risk of long-term damage. So, get trained and save lives. These words are the essence of our shared mission and our hope for a healthier, safer, and more compassionate society"

— UEFA President Aleksander Čeferin

TEST YOUR EURO KNOWLEDGE

1. For which team did Daniel Güiza score in a 2008 semi-final?

2. The 1972 semi-finals took place in Brussels and which other Belgian city?

3. When the Netherlands and Denmark met in a 1992 semi-final, who was the only player not to score his penalty in the shoot-out?

4. Which team did Yugoslavia beat 5-4 in a 1960 semi-final?

5. Which team made their first appearance in a semi-final in 2016, losing 2-0 to Portugal?

6. Who scored West Germany's penalty in their 1988 semi-final defeat by the Netherlands?

7. Which team did West Germany's Dieter Müller score a semi-final hat-trick against in 1976?

8. Anders Frisk refereed the semi-final between Portugal and the Netherlands in 2004. Which country is he from?

9. In which edition of the UEFA European Championship were there no semi-finals?

10. Amancio Amaro scored the winner for Spain in a 1964 semi-final against Hungary. Which Spanish club was he playing for at the time?

11. Who saved a Harry Kane penalty in the UEFA EURO 2020 semi-final between England and Denmark?

MISSING TEAM-MATES

Can you guess which three names are missing from England's starting line-up from their semi-final with Denmark at UEFA EURO 2020?

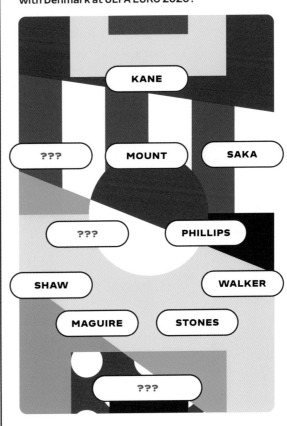

KANE

???   MOUNT   SAKA

???   PHILLIPS

SHAW   WALKER

MAGUIRE   STONES

???

12. Which future international coach scored Germany's only goal at Wembley in a 1996 semi-final against England?

13. How many goals were scored across both semi-finals in 1968?

14. Which legendary defender was the only Italian to miss in the semi-final shoot-out against the Netherlands in 2000, but still ended up on the winning side?

15. In which French city is the Stade de Gerland, the venue for the 1984 semi-final between Denmark and Spain?

YOUNGEST TO OLDEST

Can you put these EURO-winning coaches in order of age – youngest to oldest?

ROBERTO MANCINI

FERNANDO SANTOS

OTTO REHHAGEL

VICENTE DEL BOSQUE

ROGER LEMERRE

UEFA EURO 2024
MATCH SCHEDULE

EURO 2024 — GERMANY

Groups

GROUP A	GROUP B	GROUP C	GROUP D	GROUP E	GROUP F
GERMANY (GER)	SPAIN (ESP)	SLOVENIA (SVN)	POLAND (POL)	BELGIUM (BEL)	TÜRKIYE (TUR)
SCOTLAND (SCO)	CROATIA (CRO)	DENMARK (DEN)	NETHERLANDS (NED)	SLOVAKIA (SVK)	GEORGIA (GEO)
HUNGARY (HUN)	ITALY (ITA)	SERBIA (SRB)	AUSTRIA (AUT)	ROMANIA (ROU)	PORTUGAL (POR)
SWITZERLAND (SUI)	ALBANIA (ALB)	ENGLAND (ENG)	FRANCE (FRA)	UKRAINE (UKR)	CZECHIA (CZE)

Venues

Venue	Stadium	Capacity
BERLIN	Olympiastadion Berlin	71,000
LEIPZIG	Leipzig Stadium	40,000
HAMBURG	Volksparkstadion Hamburg	49,000
DORTMUND	BVB Stadion Dortmund	62,000
GELSENKIRCHEN	Arena AufSchalke	50,000
DÜSSELDORF	Düsseldorf Arena	47,000
COLOGNE	Cologne Stadium	43,000
FRANKFURT	Frankfurt Arena	47,000
STUTTGART	Stuttgart Arena	51,000
MUNICH	Munich Football Arena	66,000

Group Stage

No.	Date	Kick-off	Match	Venue
1	Fri 14.06	21:00	GER v SCO	Munich
2	Sat 15.06	15:00	HUN v SUI	Cologne
3	Sat 15.06	18:00	ESP v CRO	Berlin
4	Sat 15.06	21:00	ITA v ALB	Dortmund
5	Sun 16.06	15:00	POL v NED	Hamburg
6	Sun 16.06	18:00	SVN v DEN	Stuttgart
7	Sun 16.06	21:00	SRB v ENG	Gelsenkirchen
8	Mon 17.06	15:00	ROU v UKR	Munich
9	Mon 17.06	18:00	BEL v SVK	Frankfurt
10	Mon 17.06	21:00	AUT v FRA	Düsseldorf
11	Tue 18.06	18:00	TUR v GEO	Dortmund
12	Tue 18.06	21:00	POR v CZE	Leipzig
13	Wed 19.06	15:00	CRO v ALB	Hamburg
14	Wed 19.06	18:00	GER v HUN	Stuttgart
15	Wed 19.06	21:00	SCO v SUI	Cologne
16	Thu 20.06	15:00	SVN v SRB	Munich
17	Thu 20.06	18:00	DEN v ENG	Frankfurt
18	Thu 20.06	21:00	ESP v ITA	Gelsenkirchen
19	Fri 21.06	15:00	SVK v UKR	Düsseldorf
20	Fri 21.06	18:00	POL v AUT	Berlin
21	Fri 21.06	21:00	NED v FRA	Leipzig
22	Sat 22.06	15:00	GEO v CZE	Hamburg
23	Sat 22.06	18:00	TUR v POR	Dortmund
24	Sat 22.06	21:00	BEL v ROU	Cologne
25	Sun 23.06	21:00	SUI v GER	Frankfurt
26	Sun 23.06	21:00	SCO v HUN	Stuttgart
27	Mon 24.06	21:00	CRO v ITA	Leipzig
28	Mon 24.06	21:00	ALB v ESP	Düsseldorf
29	Tue 25.06	18:00	NED v AUT	Berlin
30	Tue 25.06	18:00	FRA v POL	Dortmund
31	Tue 25.06	21:00	ENG v SVN	Cologne
32	Tue 25.06	21:00	DEN v SRB	Munich
33	Wed 26.06	18:00	SVK v ROU	Frankfurt
34	Wed 26.06	18:00	UKR v BEL	Stuttgart
35	Wed 26.06	21:00	CZE v TUR	Hamburg
36	Wed 26.06	21:00	GEO v POR	Gelsenkirchen

Knockout Stage

Round of 16

Date	Kick-off	Match	Venue
Sat 29.06	18:00	2A v 2B	Berlin
Sat 29.06	21:00	1A v 2C	Dortmund
Sun 30.06	18:00	1C v 3D/E/F	Gelsenkirchen
Sun 30.06	21:00	1B v 3A/D/E/F	Cologne
Mon 01.07	18:00	2D v 2E	Düsseldorf
Mon 01.07	21:00	1F v 3A/B/C	Frankfurt
Tue 02.07	18:00	1E v 3A/B/C/D	Munich
Tue 02.07	21:00	1D v 2F	Leipzig

Quarter-Finals

Date	Kick-off	Match	Venue
Fri 05.07	18:00	W39 v W37	Stuttgart
Fri 05.07	21:00	W41 v W42	Hamburg
Sat 06.07	18:00	W40 v W38	Düsseldorf
Sat 06.07	21:00	W43 v W44	Berlin

Semi-Finals

Date	Kick-off	Match	Venue
Tue 09.07	21:00	W45 v W46	Munich
Wed 10.07	21:00	W47 v W48	Dortmund

Final

Date	Kick-off	Match	Venue
Sun 14.07	21:00	51 — W49 v W50	Berlin

Rest Days: 27.06 / 28.06 · 03.07 / 04.07 · 07.07 / 08.07 · 11.07 / 12.07 / 13.07